THE HISTORY OF MODERN MUSIC

THE HISTORY OF MODERN MUSIC

A COURSE OF LECTURES DELIVERED AT THE ROYAL INSTITUTION OF GREAT BRITAIN

JOHN HULLAH

GYAN

Published by

GYAN

Gyan Publishing House
5, Ansari Road
Daryaganj, New Delhi-110002
Phone: 011-47034999, 9811692060
E-mail: books@gyanbooks.com

Distribution Network
gyanbooks.com
India, USA, Canada, UK, Australia

ISBN: 978-93-7225-060-2 (PB)

First Published, 1875

2nd Impression 2026

Printed at: Gyan Press, Delhi.

THE HISTORY OF MODERN MUSIC
Author: JOHN HULLAH

THE HISTORY OF MODERN MUSIC

THE

HISTORY OF MODERN MUSIC.

A Course of Lectures

DELIVERED AT THE

ROYAL INSTITUTION OF GREAT BRITAIN.

BY

JOHN HULLAH, LL.D.

Io non posso ritrar di tutti appieno,
Perocchè si mi caccia il lungo tema,
Che molte volte al fatto il dir vien meno.
DANTE.

SIXTH EDITION.

LONDON
LONGMANS, GREEN AND CO.
AND NEW YORK: 15 EAST 16th STREET
1891

TO

ARTHUR HELPS, Esq.

This Book

IS GRATEFULLY AND AFFECTIONATELY INSCRIBED

BY

THE AUTHOR

PREFACE

TO

THE FIRST EDITION.

THIS volume contains the substance of a Course of Lectures delivered at the Royal Institution in the early part of this present year.* I have explained in the first Lecture the motives which dictated my choice of subject; in its treatment I have kept two objects constantly in view.

(1) To bring out and illustrate that great change in the idiom of Modern Music which accompanied or followed the Renaissance; and to show how far this change differed, in kind and in extent, from that produced on the Sister Arts by the same agency. I do not think that this can be said to have been done, or even attempted, before,—within the same limits, or in any connected manner. The musical student desiring information on the subject has been hitherto compelled to seek it at a number of sources, often difficult of access, and not always very satisfactory when reached.

(2) In connexion with this I have tried to awaken some interest and curiosity among my hearers (or readers), in what may be briefly described as "unknown music." Without wishing for a moment to lower in public estimation such composers as have attained, and still maintain, the greatest favour, I cannot but think that the attention which they continue exclusively to

* 1862.

receive might, with no detriment to them, and with great advantage to the world, be occasionally extended to others; and (which is less likely to be questioned) that where that attention has been limited (as in most cases it has been) to a few of their productions, it might, with equal advantage, be spread over many. Our English musical societies, of whatever kind—even the most prosperous and independent of them—are condemned, by public indifference, to a small cycle of works, the repetition of which year after year, becomes beyond measure wearisome to those on whom it devolves, and (which is a more serious consideration) acts as a discouragement on the creative faculty,—the certain, though perhaps indirect, result of which must be the deterioration of any art in all its branches. It is not more difficult to awaken public sympathy with an unknown composer, be he old or new, than to find an audience for an unknown composition, be its author never so well known or so popular. Should the English musical public ever break through the wall with which it has allowed apathy and prejudice to "protect" it from "the fresh woods and pastures new" which lie untrodden on its outer side, assuredly a thousand new instances will present themselves of the truth contained in the poet's line, now passed into a proverb—

The world knows nothing of its greatest men.

The pursuit of the former and more important of the two objects of these Lectures was manifestly inconsistent with much mere biographical detail. It might have been possible, even within the time and space at my disposal, to name many more persons and to allude to many more things than will be found named or alluded to in the following pages; but the result would inevitably have been one of those "Abstracts of History" which are notoriously the hardest of all hard reading, and of the contents of which few memories are strong enough to retain any useful impression, general or particular.

The division which I have made into Periods will, I trust, help the reader to keep the epochs, positive and relative, of individual great Masters in his mind. These periods, as I have more than once shown, are not distinguished or limited by mere external musical forms, (the successive varieties of which no imaginable number of periods would suffice to classify,) but by the nature of the material of which those forms are composed—technically their "tonality." Strictly speaking, Modern Music knows but *two* Periods—that ending with the epoch of Palestrina, and that in which we live; but the long years of preparation for the former, and of transition from it to the latter, demanded places which could not with propriety be assigned to them within either.

The Chronological Tables at the end of the volume are reduced copies of diagrams which I kept before my auditors during the delivery of these Lectures. Besides their obvious utility as means for comparing the epochs of different composers—better, because more graphic than the mere enumeration of dates,—they present, if not a complete list of musical composers, at any rate the names of the majority of those who, by some special and individual effort, have had an appreciable influence, be it more or less, on the progress of their art.

J. H

December, 1861.

PREFACE

TO

THE SECOND EDITION.

The volume prefaced by the foregoing has been out of print about ten years, during which such increasingly frequent calls for copies of it have been made that, more pressing occupation preventing the preparation of a new edition, I have many times been on the point of sanctioning a reprint of the old one. I cannot but rejoice at not having done this. A course of six Lectures only, no one of which was to exceed an hour in delivery, on a subject so extended as the History of Modern Music was inevitably a very incomplete course. Moreover the trenchant brevity with which many questions were of necessity treated in it resulted, as I have since found, in false impressions of my opinions in respect to them.

The present issue has afforded me the opportunity of supplying some at least of the gravest omissions from the former one; and though the book itself be still far from what a much enlarged plan, and leisure such as it has never been my lot to enjoy, might have enabled me to make it—for History is not to be written in the intervals of "more important" occupations—I would willingly hope that from the "outlines" before the reader no important particular is omitted, and that he may be enabled to form from them a tolerably accurate idea of the progress of Modern Music from its beginnings to the present time. Details, in respect either to musical persons or things, are, especially to those who read French or German, easily accessible. In any case I have repeatedly disclaimed any intention of presenting them.

The dedication is left as it originally stood. The valued friend by whom it was accepted has, only within this present year, gone to his rest,—hardly less mourned by those who knew him only through his writings than by those who were privileged, by closer contact, to estimate the large benevolence, the disciplined intellect and the profound and varied acquirements of which those writings were the outcome and the expression. His services to his Sovereign and his Country were, as is well known, not unrecognised; and could the dedication, like the book which follows it, be revised, it would present a striking record of the estimation in which he was held by both.

J. H.

November, 1875.

CONTENTS.

LECTURE I.

PAGE

THE FIRST PERIOD (from *cir.* 370 to *cir.* 1400) 1

LECTURE II.

THE SECOND PERIOD (from *cir.* 1400 to *cir.* 1600) 37

LECTURE III.

THE THIRD PERIOD (from *cir.* 1600 to *cir.* 1750) 73

LECTURE IV.

THE THIRD PERIOD (*continued*) 99

LECTURE V.

THE FOURTH PERIOD (from *cir.* 1750 to the present time) . . . 137

LECTURE VI.

THE FOURTH PERIOD (*continued*) 169

LECTURE VII.

THE FOURTH PERIOD (*continued*) 191

THE

HISTORY OF MODERN MUSIC.

THE FIRST PERIOD.

FROM ABOUT A.D. 370 TO ABOUT A.D. 1400.

INTRODUCTORY—MUSICAL SYSTEM—MODERN MUSIC—THE NATIONS THAT HAVE CONTRIBUTED TO ITS PROGRESS—THE FOUR PERIODS OF ITS HISTORY—EARLY CHRISTIAN MUSIC—ITS SOURCES—ITS PERFORMANCE—CONGREGATIONAL SINGING—SINGING SCHOOLS—THE AUTHENTIC MODES—ST. AMBROSE—GREGORY THE GREAT—MUSICAL NOTATION—ISIDORE OF SEVILLE—HUCBALD—HARMONY—ITS NORTHERN ORIGIN—ANCIENT BOWED INSTRUMENTS—THE CRWTH—HUCBALD'S EXAMPLES OF DIAPHONY—GUIDO ARETINO—HIS INVENTIONS—SOLMISATION—MEDIÆVAL MUSIC—CANTUS MENSURABILIS—THE PROSE OF MONTPELLIER—SECULAR MEDIÆVAL MELODY—SPECIMENS—DESCANT—THE TIME-TABLE—FRANCO OF COLOGNE—LAST YEARS OF THE TWELFTH AND FIRST OF THE THIRTEENTH CENTURIES—END OF THE FIRST PERIOD.

THE FIRST PERIOD.

I PROPOSE, during the course on which we enter to-day, to bring under your notice some outlines of modern musical history. I say "outlines;" for the presentation of anything like detail in respect to so large a subject—a subject involving so much of fact and of speculation, so many names, and so many works—would, I am sure, prove impracticable within the time allotted to me. "Would it be possible," wrote the Editor of the "Cabinet Cyclopædia" to M. de Sismondi, "to comprise the history of the Italian Republics in one small volume?" I have many times put a similar question to myself. Will it be possible to present, in any intelligible form, the History of Modern Music in six hours? Perhaps a more entertaining course, certainly one more easy to myself, might have been made by taking as a subject some one of those epochs at which great changes have come over the musical art, or some one or two of the artists by whom those changes have been carried out. But, though possibly more entertaining, I do not think that such a course would have been so useful as that which I have decided on giving. A very little intercourse with society is needed to prove that not so much incorrect views as no views at all prevail very generally, in respect to the history, especially the early history, of an art which so many now love so dearly and practise so skilfully. Nor is this indifference to the past at all confined to those who cultivate music solely as a recreation. Very accomplished musicians, composers equally with performers, are often absolutely ignorant of the works, epochs, nay, the very names, of some of those who have exercised the greatest influence on the progress of the art whose culture is the business of their own lives. If in this particular musicians present an exception to all other contemporary artists their condition may be accounted for, if not excused.

Poetry, architecture, sculpture and painting have severally attained to excellence which there can be no reasonable hope of surpassing, at one or more periods comparatively remote from us. But music is a new art. I do not mean that music literally began to have a being in this or the last century, or in the century before that. Who shall say when men did without something they at least called music? But what we now call music, that which completely realizes our idea of, answers to our definition of, music, has come into being only within comparatively few years; almost within the memory of men living. Take the case of the noblest form of instrumental music, the Symphony for full orchestra; in its greatest perfection exhibited in the works of this kind of Beethoven. Beethoven died as recently as 1827; any man now in middle life, therefore, might have seen him; indeed some of his pupils are still among us.* Nay, more, not only have men living witnessed the development and perfection of this form of composition, but its youth, almost its infancy. One† certainly, perhaps more than one, of these played at Salomon's Concerts (in 1791) when the well-known "Twelve Symphonies" of Haydn were first produced, under the direction of their composer.

Do not let us fall too hardly then on the modern musician for his ignorance or indifference about his predecessors. Like the Gothic architects of the fourteenth century, and the painters of the fifteenth and sixteenth, the musical composers and performers of the eighteenth and nineteenth cen-

* This was literally true. Mr. Cipriani Potter attended this course of lectures, delivered in 1861.

† Sir George Smart.

turies have been too much occupied in making history, to study it.

But I must not seem to depreciate the subject in which it is my wish to give you an interest, such interest as is due from persons of general culture and lively sympathies, in what has, in some form or other, been a joy and a consolation to every people, in every age. Music, modern music especially, is beyond all question a much finer thing than anything that is in the least likely ever to be said about it. But a good deal is to be said about it which ought to be worthy of attention; and if its history is not made interesting, it must be because of the way in which it is presented, or because those who read it or listen to it, do so with so little preparation that it is impossible to address them in intelligible terms. I hope I may take it for granted that those whom I have the honour to address now have some acquaintance with at least the rudiments of musical science. To expect more would be unreasonable. I will try to be as untechnical as I can; but without being a little technical, I could not hope to make myself intelligible, or indeed to be of the smallest use to you.

The history of modern music is really comprised in comparatively few years. For, although it would be inexcusable to omit from the baldest outline of it certain grand forms which loom out of the darkness of the earlier centuries of our era, yet we shall find little demanding precise presentation before the eleventh century; and little of what we now understand by music, before the fifteenth century. Moreover, the history of modern music is altogether European. Not that the Orientals have, or have had, no music of their own; but that, as at present practised, their music has no charm, nor indeed meaning, for us. How is this? How can there be music acceptable to one comparatively civilized people and altogether unacceptable, unintelligible even, to another? The answer is to be found in the different nature of their musical "system;"

a word which, as applied to music, I shall best define by reading you a passage which I have translated from an able French writer.

"M. Villoteau, a musician formerly attached to the French Opera, was among the number of *Savans* who accompanied Bonaparte in his expedition to Egypt. His occupation was to collect information about the music of the various Orientals who are to be found in that country. On his arrival at Cairo, he placed himself under an Arabian music master, whose lessons consisted in teaching his pupil to sing certain airs by ear and from memory; for in Egypt he is the most approved artist who knows the greatest number of tunes by heart. M. Villoteau, who proposed to collect all the national melodies he could find, set to work to write, under the dictation of his instructor; and observing, while he wrote, that the intonation of the latter was occasionally false, he took care to allow for his (supposed) inaccuracies, and to put on paper not exactly what his instructor sang, which indeed in our notation would have been impossible, but what it might be supposed he had meant to sing. This operation ended, M. Villoteau proceeded to test practically the accuracy of his own work; but the Arab stopped him in the middle of the first phrase, telling him that he (M. Villoteau) was singing out of tune. Thereupon followed a very lively discussion between master and pupil; each maintaining that his own intonation was unimpeachable, and neither allowing the other to sing half a dozen notes without protest. At last it occurred to M. Villoteau that there must be something in this discrepancy which required closer investigation. He procured a lute of native facture, the finger-board of which was divided (by *frets*), according to the rules of the Arabian musical scale. The mystery was explained in a moment. An inspection of this instrument showed him, to his great surprise, that the very elements of the music with which he was familiar, and those of the music with which he desired to make acquaintance, were absolutely different. The intervals of the two scales were dissimilar, and the education of the European musician made it as difficult for him to seize or appreciate Arabian melody as to execute it."*

I shall have occasion, in another lecture, to allude to the various modes, or forms of scale, used in the fifteenth and sixteenth centuries. It is difficult enough for an ear trained in the nineteenth century, to reconcile itself to some of these. But to reconcile itself to another "system" seems not so much difficult as impossible. Happily it is not in the least necessary. The modern European system, though the exigences of practice prevent its being absolutely true, is nearer the truth than any other; and its inaccuracies are so slight as to cause little disturbance to the most refined ear. I mean by this that all our music is of necessity a little out of tune; for some of our intervals vary, however slightly, from those deduced from the division of a musical string into aliquot parts. But the discrepancy is so slight, and distributed by "equal temperament" over so many instances, that it is practically of no consequence.

To return. Not only does the history of modern music concern Europe only, but a very small portion of it. For though it is impossible to name any European people which has not contributed somebody or something to the progress of the art, that progress has been due chiefly to three nations :—the Belgians and Northern French, who as regards this subject must be considered as one people, and of whom I shall speak for the future as the Gallo-Belgians, the Italians, the Germans, and more recently the French. Doubtless we (English) have had, from an early period, a school, and a great one, of our own. Spain too has not been without its composers and performers; and Russia and Scandinavia are, and have long been, musical nations. But it would be hard to prove that any one

* Fétis, "Biographie Universelle des Musiciens." Bruxelles, 1837, tom. i. p. xl.

of these nations has contributed directly to the progress of the art; or that the art would have been other than it is, if none of them had ever practised it. It is a little mortifying to ourselves, but no less true, that foreigners "make a point" of ignoring our existence as a musical people. Of the works of English musicians little is known in Germany, nothing in France and Italy. Foreign musical histories, dictionaries and periodicals, when they notice us at all, which is not often, are pretty sure to tell their readers something or other about us which is not true. They misspell our names, credit us with works to which we have no claim, and kill us years before our time.

The history of modern music may be conveniently divided into four Periods. During the First there was little produced of any interest, other than historical, to the musician. But as a period in the history of the world is commonly assigned to its formation out of Chaos, so a period in Musical History seems due to those experiments in sound the result of which is what we now call music, and to those attempts at representing sound to which we owe modern notation. No date can be safely assigned to the beginning of this First Period; but it may be considered to have ended about the year 1400. The Second Period extends from this date to about the year 1600; the Third to about 1750. In the Fourth we are now living.

These Periods may be thus described:—the First, as a period of preparation; the Second, as that of the old tonality, and of (to us) the old masters; the Fourth, as that of the modern tonality, and the modern school; and the Third as a transition period from the Second to the Fourth.

The boundary lines of these Periods you will find, here and there, somewhat devious and faint. One musician may have to be included in a period which had nominally ended ere his career was fairly begun. For another it is hard to find a place at all; such an anachronism does he present. But on a moment's reflection, you will cease to wonder at this; seeing that in all ages there have been men before, as well as men behind, their age; prospective, as well as retrospective, men. The most striking examples of this latter class are to be found, appropriately enough, in the Roman School. The Roman School attained its highest development in the second half of the sixteenth century. It does not so much belong to as constitute the Second Period. Yet it can scarcely be said to have expired till the middle of the last century, when Pitoni, among musicians "ultimus Romanorum," finished a career which would seem to have been misplaced by two centuries. Nevertheless, with the aid of these divisions, we shall be enabled to arrange our musical chronology much better than without them. They admit, as you will find, of considerable subdivision.

The first public use of music, by every people, has been a "religious" use. The means presented by the art of amplifying and prolonging ceremonial; of raising, and of sustaining, in great multitudes, a similar state of feeling; above all, of giving simultaneous expression to this feeling, be it what it may;—all these qualities would at all times have recommended music to those on whom the arrangement of rites and ceremonies has fallen. That the early Christians loved and practised music we know from sacred as well as profane history. We are told* that Paul and Silas, when in captivity, "prayed and sang praises to God," at midnight. We know, too,† that St. Paul distinguishes singing "with the spirit," from singing "with the understanding also." The principal charge of Pliny the Younger against the Christians was, that they sang hymns to Christ as to God—"quasi Deo."

We have no authentic record, nor could such be expected, as to the kind of music in which the piety of the early Christian converts found expression. Its origin, too, in spite of diligent enquiry, is still involved in obscurity, still matter of doubt.

* Acts xvi. 25. † 1 Cor. xiv. 15.

The music of the Primitive Church may have been inherited from the Jews, or borrowed from the Greeks; or it may have been an altogether original creation, itself the result of a new faith.

In regard to the first hypothesis it has been argued that the Service of the Jewish Temple was interrupted by the Captivity; and that the Jewish melody, not being *noted,* would, on the return of the Jews to their native land, prove difficult if not impossible to recover. After the Captivity, too, the Jews became more like other people in customs and externals. The new Temple, for example, was built in the Corinthian style. Surely Greek melody might easily have found its way into it. Moreover, this difficulty even surmounted, and proof afforded that Jewish melodies were known to and used by the Apostles, how could they have been transmitted to new churches, and taught to new converts, at Ephesus, Corinth, Rome, and elsewhere? Again, the early Christians would be too anxious to steer clear of anything that might even seem like Judaism, to take what they could get from others from the Jews.

In regard to the second hypothesis it has been argued that the early, or at least earliest, converts to Christianity were for the most too poor, too simple, and too prejudiced against Greek art and life, to adopt or imitate anything belonging to either. On the other hand, it is certain that this condition of feeling or of things was not, could not be, long maintained. The Christians early participated in many indifferent heathen customs. They adopted the ram-bearing Hermes as the Good Shepherd, and used Orpheus as a symbol, if not a representation, of our Lord. They made sarcophagi of pagan forms, and adopted the Basilica, essentially a secular structure, as their first church. Prudentius wrote in the language and metre of Virgil. Then again has not the poverty and ignorance of the early Christians been exaggerated? To be "poor in spirit," in the scriptural sense, is not surely of necessity to be poor in intelligence or even in circumstances. Persons of high rank and culture were among them, to whom Greek music must have been as familiar as any other art. Why should they have forgotten or refused to use heathen *melody* only, availing themselves as they did of heathen architecture, sculpture, and painting, and conforming to heathen customs involving no matters of principle?

The third hypothesis may be dismissed as inconsistent with all experience.

The music of the early Church was no doubt simple; it was certainly unaccompanied. The instruments available for accompaniment were few. One of these, the lyre, subsequently a Christian symbol, was in early times essentially a mundane instrument; the other, the tibia, was used in, and therefore closely associated with, heathen sacrifices. Both instruments served as accompaniments to pantomime. Feeling too might dictate, prudence assuredly would, the suppression or avoidance of any considerable amount of musical intensity, as being likely to attract attention, for a time sure to be followed by persecution.

Simple as this music might be, the modes of performing it were very various. Hymns were sung in the Christian assemblies by a single voice; by the whole congregation; by the congregation antiphonally; and by a single voice antiphonally with the congregation. It is possible that the antiphonal division of the entire congregation was made according to sex, a division maintained in many places to our own time, and as convenient as it is favourable to musical effect; the voices of the two sexes differing in pitch by an octave.

The conversion of Constantine had a great effect on the music of his age. Both the Emperor and his mother Helena actively promoted the building of churches. Noble structures rose, chiefly through their instrumentality, in Jerusalem, Rome, Ravenna, Constantinople, and other cities. A ritual at all in keeping with these involved of necessity music more elaborate than had been known before, and with it a class or order to execute it. Difficulties about what is called "congregational singing" have not originated in post-reformation times. They date at least from the fourth century. No means presented itself to the Council of Laodicea (c. 315) of securing decency and order in public worship, but forbidding the laity to sing in church at all. Their decree, however regarded, indicates the existence of some kind of musical culture. Whatever might be the musical standard of excellence among the clergy of the fourth century, they must have had one, and tried by it the laity must have been found wanting.

In the beginning of the fourth century Pope Sylvester founded a singing school in Rome; the earliest of which we have record. Another school was founded a little later by Hilarius, at Poictiers, the scholars of which were taken, very young, from the Orphanage.*

In these schools, and in this century, were formalized the "authentic modes;" a set of scales or portions of scales beginning severally on the sounds D, E, F, and G. It is possible that these modes had, in the minds of those who selected and formalized them, some mystic affinity with the four Evangelists. Tradition ascribes their choice, and even arrangement, to St. Ambrose (elected Bishop of Milan in 374), whose name they still bear. To what extent the Church is indebted to the personal efforts of St. Ambrose in this re-formation or formation of the music of his time it would be hard to say. Certain it is that Church music was then far better at Milan than at Rome; and that, during his episcopacy, antiphonal singing was first sanctioned in Western Europe. Augustine, himself a musician, pays an eloquent tribute to the touching beauty of the Milanese music in the time of Ambrose.

* A proposition to found a similar school in London, in connexion with the "Foundling" Hospital, was made in the last century—fourteen hundred years later—by Dr. Burney, the musical historian.

"How did I weep, in Thy hymns and canticles, touched to the quick by the voices of Thy sweet-attuned Church! The voices flowed into mine ears, and the Truth distilled into my heart, whence the affections of my devotions overflowed, and tears ran down, and happy was I therein.

"Not long had the Church of Milan begun to use this kind of consolation and exhortation, the brethren zealously joining with harmony of voice and hearts. . . . . Then it was first instituted that hymns and psalms should be sung after the manner of Eastern Churches (*i.e.* antiphonally), lest the people should wax faint through the tediousness of sorrow; and from that day to this the custom is retained; divers, yea, almost all, Thy congregations throughout other parts of the world following herein."*

St. Ambrose may be regarded as the father of the Music of the Western Church. His reputation has been somewhat obscured by that of Gregory the Great, whose epoch is two centuries nearer to our own. But though the labours of Ambrose may not have been so beneficial to the Church and to the world as those of Gregory, they are even more honourable to himself, as having been effected under incomparably greater difficulties. For not only had Ambrose to adapt music to the different portions of the Church Service, but to determine and define, almost to form, the musical idiom in which it was to be cast. Like the great Florentine poet of a later age, he had to create an instrument wherewith to do his work; that instrument being nothing less than a language.

I have already spoken of the difficulty we all have in imagining a musical "system" other than that to which we are used. Similar difficulty, though in a less degree, is felt in respect to any "tonality," or arrangement of the sounds of our system, other than that in which all modern music is composed. I shall enter somewhat fully into this matter in another lecture.

* Conf. B. ix. s. 15.

Suffice it for the moment that Ambrose had to select from the only source open to him, Greek Music, in the best of times intricate, and in his all but inexplicable, a set of scales, "modes" or "tones," few enough and simple enough for the use of a very rude people.

The second of these four scales or "tones," is formed by the succession of two Greek "tetrachords;" while the first and fourth present all the forms of tetrachord possible. The tetrachord, the basis of all melody, consists of four sounds separated by two tones and one semitone; it admits therefore of only three varieties, those afforded by the position of this one semitone. The Greek tetrachord, that in which the semitone occupies the lowest place, includes both the modern 7th sound or leading-note, which designates the "key" in which every passage is said to be, and the 3rd sound, which designates the "mode" of that key. E is the leading note, and A the 3rd of the key of F; the first tetrachord of the second tone is therefore in F. B is the leading note, and E the 3rd of C; the second tetrachord of the second tone is therefore in C.

Fig. 1.

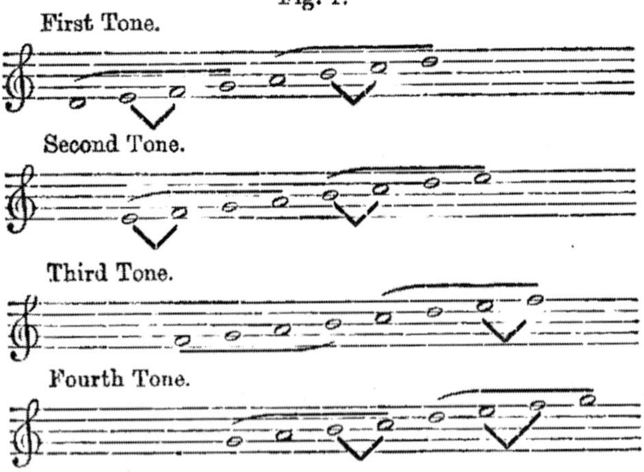

The two tetrachords of the first tone are of like construction, the semitone in each falls between the 2nd and 3rd sounds.

So in the second tone, only that the semitone in each falls between the 1st and 2nd sounds. In the fourth tone the semitone falls between the 3rd and 4th sounds of the first tetrachord, and the 2nd and 3rd of the second. The third tone presents the anomaly—the "diabolus in musica" of the Middle Ages—of a "tritone," or succession of three tones, occupying the place of the first tetrachord. The necessity for remedying this led early to the substitution of B flat for B natural; as subsequently the necessity for making the two tetrachords of the fourth tone alike led to the substitution of F sharp for F natural. I shall return to this subject later. Meanwhile you will observe that the one substitution I have named in each of the last two tones, would make both conformable to modern tonality; whereas alterations much more considerable would be needed to produce the same effect in either of the first two.

I will only add that in the use of the monotone "quantity" was carefully observed in Ambrosian chanting; and that everything we should call melody, to which variety of pitch is as essential as variety of duration, was reserved for the endings of strains. The obligations of Ambrose to the East are evidenced in many of his institutions. *E.g.*, he called his tones *protos*, *deuteros*, *tritus*, and *tetradus*. Of Northern or "Barbarian" influence they present no trace.

During the two centuries which connect the epochs of St. Ambrose and Gregory the Great (elected 590), the institutions of the former fell, as might have been expected in such an age, into utter confusion.

Ambrose, working on Greek models, or at least taking Greek music, as far as he knew it, as his point of departure, had given much attention to prosody. By the end of the sixth century every trace of this element would seem to have been obliterated from Church music. Clergy and laity had alike got

"to scan
With Midas' ears, committing short and long."

Moreover, the limits of the Ambrosian tones, like the Roman frontier, had been so often violated that it had become doubtful where they were to be found.

Gregory began his reform of Church music by gathering together what remained of the results of the labours of Ambrose and others, with a view of recasting them into an Antiphonary, or authorized body of ecclesiastical music. He would seem, early in his labours, to have found that the Ambrosian scales were too few, and of too limited extent for his later age; and that adherence to them would have involved the exclusion of many melodies fitted, by their excellence or their popularity, for his purpose. Never was reform carried out in a bolder and at the same time more reverential spirit. Gregory did not destroy but add to the work of Ambrose; connecting with *his* four scales, which were then first distinguished by the epithet "authentic," four other subordinate or collateral scales which were called "plagal"—a word best done into English by "athwart."

From this time even to the present not only have the chants for the Psalms, still in such extensive use, borne the name of Gregory, but every variety of ecclesiastical melody also. Nay—so does a great name gather round it the waifs and strays of invention—the square notes still in use for this kind of music, though not invented till nearly six hundred years after Gregory's death, and even then not used for plain-song for another two hundred years, are universally called Gregorian notes.

Though the history of musical notation is far too large a subject for me to treat at all fully in this course of lectures, I cannot help referring to a question which I am sure must have already suggested itself to you. How was Gregory's Antiphonary written? Or, to be more precise, in what way was the musical part of it expressed? Till very recently it was commonly believed that Gregory made use of the first seven letters of the alphabet, repeated in the octave, to represent the comparatively small number of sounds used in Gregorian song. This belief may have arisen from the fact that the Romans, in imitation of the Greeks, used an alphabetic notation. No codex of the Roman liturgy, however, has been discovered in this notation, nor does any ancient writer mention it. In regard to Gregory, however, the question has been settled beyond dispute. There exists in the Monastery of St. Gall, in Switzerland, one of two copies of his Antiphonary, which was made for Peter and Romanus, two choristers sent by Pope Adrian I. to Charlemagne, to reform the northern Church music, about the year 780. A facsimile of this book,* edited by Père Lambillotte, was published a few years since. The music is written throughout above the words, not in letters, but in *neumata;* a notation in very extensive use throughout Western Christendom from the 6th to the 12th century. It first received the name by which it is now generally known from Ducange, with whom to "neume" or "neumaticize" is to note. Much research has lately been brought to bear on the origin, development, and eventual transformation of neumes into notes such as we now use, in no instance perhaps so successfully as in M. de Coussemaker's "Histoire de l'Harmonie au Moyen Age,"† a truly splendid monument of the diligence, learning and acuteness of its author; one of a class of books, too, I grieve to say, which none but men of fortune could afford either to write or to publish in England, but which, somehow or other, are written, often by men of small means, and published in the ordinary way of trade, in other countries, where, it may be supposed, they find purchasers and readers.

The labours of Gregory for the reformation and spread of music were not limited to the formation of his Antiphonary, albeit in his time a work demanding much thought and toil. He established singing schools in Rome, and not only superin-

* Bruxelles, 1867. † Paris, 1852.

tended, but took part in the teaching in, them. One of his early biographers tells us that, even when his infirmities compelled him to a recumbent posture, he continued to teach; and that the bed on which he lay, and the stick with which he beat time—or his laggard or unruly scholars—were long preserved in Rome as memorials of his enthusiasm and practicalness.

Contemporary with Gregory, who is supposed frequently to have consulted and communicated with him, was another ecclesiastical dignitary, Isidore Archbishop of Seville, a man who to his other many accomplishments added a knowledge of music. In a treatise of his which has come down to us, "Sententiæ de Musica," we find the earliest mention, yet discovered, of *Harmony* in the modern acceptation of the term—the simultaneous utterance of different sounds. Isidore speaks of two kinds of harmony, "symphony" and "diaphony;" by the former of which he would seem to have meant a combination of consonant, and by the latter of dissonant, intervals.

During the four centuries which connect the epoch of Gregory with that of Guido Aretino, only one name worthy of special mention in musical history presents itself; that of Hucbald, a monk of St. Armand in the diocese of Tournay, in Belgic Gaul, a district to which we shall often have occasion to refer as the cradle of modern music. Hucbald was a poet as well as a musician, and exhibited his talents in reference to the oddest subject, and in the oddest manner, that ever entered the mind of man. He is the author of a poem of more than a hundred lines* in praise of baldness, "Ægloga de Calvis," every word of which begins with the letter C. I will give you the first line—

> Carmina clarisonæ calvis cantate Camæne.

and the two last—

> Conveniet claras claustris componere cannas,
> Completur claris carmen cantabile calvis.

* It may be found entire in the "Adversaria" of Barthius, lib. xlvi. cap. xxii. p. 2175.

He dedicated this astonishing production, appropriately enough, to Charles the Bald of France.

Hucbald died at an advanced age in the year 932. The two of his treatises which have been preserved give us a sufficiently complete idea of the condition of polyphonic music up to the commencement of the tenth century. It is certain, as we have seen, that some kind of harmony had appeared in Italy, and even made its way into the services of the Church long before this; before even the time of Gregory, perhaps even in that of Ambrose. Nor is it possible to trace this harmony to any but a Northern source; seeing that evidence has been found to prove that, time immemorial, the inhabitants of Northern Europe have known the use of instruments capable of producing, and indeed hardly to be used without producing, different sounds at the same instant of time. Not to speak of the innumerable varieties of harp and guitar, instruments of which the strings are pulled by the finger or by a plectrum of some kind, the origin of which is lost in antiquity, an instrument has been in use for ages past, both in Russia and in our own country, mounted with three or more strings, and played upon with a bow, but differing from all our violin tribe in this essential particular, that the sides not being *échancrées*, or hollowed out to admit the passage of the bow, and the bridge being flat, not arched, all three or more strings must inevitably be sounded at once. In the Russian instrument the strings are said to have been tuned harmonically, the second string being the 5th, and the third the 8ve to the first. The English, or rather *British* instrument, the *crwth* or crowd (Lat. *crotta*), had, in its most recent condition, six strings. A paper by the Hon. Daines Barrington, read at the Society of Antiquaries, May 3rd, 1770,* describes minutely a crwth which, though not individually of great antiquity, might have been reasonably regarded as only a somewhat improved specimen of a class which

* See "Archælogia," vol. iii. p. 32.

had been common in Wales for centuries before. This paper is illustrated by a drawing of which Fig. 2 is a facsimile. The pitch, or "tuning" of the strings is given below it. The drawing, though rude and incorrect, exhibits the peculiarities of the instrument, and explains how it was used. The fingers of the player's left hand were passed through the aperture above the finger-board, the thumb through that below it. The two thickest strings were drones, or *bourdons,* whose pitch was unalterable save by tuning; but the other four admitted every variety of intonation possible without "shifting" the hand. One foot of the bridge, which is placed athwart the body of the instrument, is projected so far as to be connected with the sound-post, which is visible through the lower sound-hole. But what chiefly concerns us now is the fact insisted on in the paper, that "the bridge of the crwth is perfectly flat, so that all the strings are necessarily struck [with the bow] at the same time, and afford a *perpetual succession of chords.*"

Fig. 2.

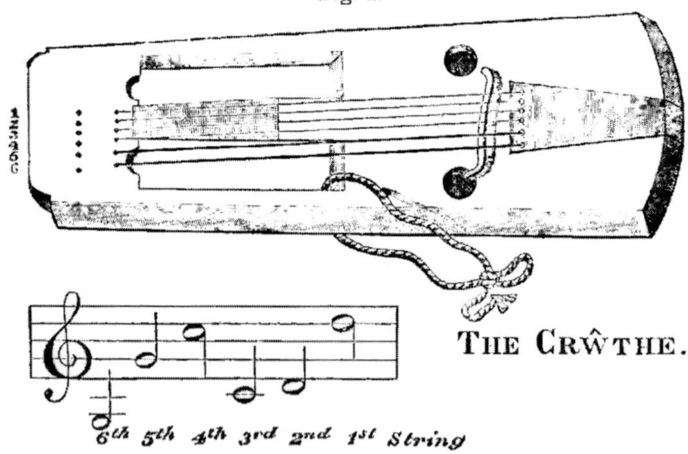

Examples of bowed instruments, varying in other respects, but so formed that, like the crwth, "all the strings are necessarily struck at the same time," are numerous in mediæval manuscripts and sculpture.

If we take into consideration this necessity (for the simultaneous vibration of strings of different pitch) in respect to bowed instruments, the use of which among northern nations is lost in antiquity, in connexion with the fact that the earliest mention of harmony (by Isidore) is a little subsequent to the first barbarian invasions of the South of Europe, we are driven to the conclusion that we owe to the same people harmony, and the glorious architecture of the Middle Ages; and that the former is equally with the latter a Gothic, in contradistinction to a Classic, form of art.

To return however to Hucbald. He not only mentions, but gives us examples of the "harmony" of his age—*diaphony*, or *organum*. There were several kinds of organum; and hideous, intolerable as most of them may be to our ears, some of the worst are theoretically justifiable by the now well-ascertained and universally acknowledged laws of physical science; laws to the judicious observance of which the noblest and most complicated of musical instruments, the organ, owes all its peculiarities and all its pre-eminence.

But you shall judge of these forms of organum for yourselves.

In Hucbald's treatise a melody to be harmonized is called *vox principalis*, or *principalis;* and the part added, *vox organalis*, or *organalis*. A *principalis* could be accompanied in the following different ways:—with the 8th above or below; with the 5th above; with the 4th above; with the 4th above and the 5th below; with the 5th above and the 4th below.

An example of each of these forms, in musical notation, will make this clear. I will play them in succession.

See Fig. 3. The *principalis* is given in each example in white notes; the *organum* in black notes.

EXAMPLES OF DIAPHONY OR ORGANUM.

FROM HUCBALD'S *Musica Enchiriadis.*

Fig. 3.

More than one musical historian has altogether discredited the possibility of any but the first of these forms having ever been practised by human voices, or tolerated by human ears. And were the effect of them inevitably that which is produced by playing them on a pianoforte, as I have been obliged to do, I should certainly partake in this incredulity. Such, however, is by no means inevitably the case. I can imagine more than one of them so performed as to produce something like the effect of the "mixtures" of an organ. It must be remembered that these last are only made endurable by their different intensity; a similar disposition as to voices may have been common in the Middle Ages; the mass of a congregation singing the *principalis*, and a few voices only the *organalis*.

I come now to the greatest musical name of the early Middle Ages, that of Guido Aretino or Guy of Arezzo, of whom we hear first, early in the eleventh century, as resident in the Benedictine monastery of Pomposa, between Ferrara and Ravenna. To this very ingenious person, as to Gregory, many discoveries and contrivances have been attributed to which he could have had no claim; some of them having been made before his time, and some not being alluded to in any known copy of his works. It is needless to particularize these; for those of his achievements about which there is no reason to doubt are numerous and important enough to render his name honourable among musicians to all time.

Guido Aretino may be regarded as the father of all music-masters; apparently the first teacher who ever brought musical science to bear directly on musical art; the first who ever showed any understanding of what the practical difficulties of music really are and, I may add, always will be; and the first who showed any desire to lessen or remove them. There are many difficulties connected with the musical art; but there is one paramount to all others, and which may be briefly described as *hearing with the eye*, or (its converse) *seeing with the ear*. I mean, the knowing the *sound* of a musical passage by the *sight* of the characters which represent it; or (conversely again) the power of writing it, from musical performance. To be able to do these things is to be a musician; and Guido was the first to grasp this truth. Up to his time the formation of a chorister is said to have been the work of years; he made it the work of a few months. He anticipated, by eight centuries, a method of teaching known as Jacotot's, or "the analytic," method. This consists, as applied to music, in taking any melody familiar to those who are to be taught, and fixing the sounds and intervals of which it is formed on the memory, in connexion with their representative signs; so that when the eye encounters similar signs in another melody, the ear may associate similar sounds and intervals with them. A modern musician teaching in this way might take such a melody as the well known *Adeste Fideles* (Fig. 4), the beginning of which presents types of the intervals *fourth, fifth,* and *sixth.*

Fig. 4.

One air used in teaching by Guido was so admirably adapted for carrying out this "analytic" method, that it is not at all unlikely that the system itself was suggested by it. It was the melody to which a hymn to John the Baptist (ancient even in those days) was sung. The same melody has recently turned up in connexion with other words. It is before you. (Fig. 5.)

HYMN TO JOHN THE BAPTIST.

Fig. 5.

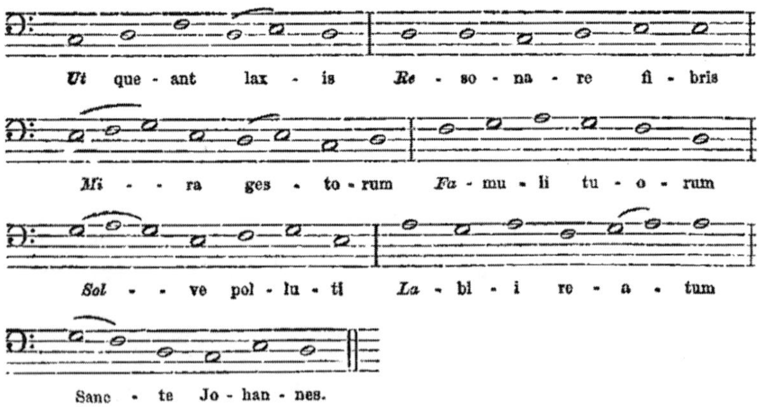

Now this melody, the merits of which we will not stop to discuss, offers the remarkable peculiarity that the first syllable of every verse, or line, is sung to a note one degree higher than that sung to the first syllable of the verse before it; in other words, the several first sounds of each phrase presented successively would form "a scale." Guido's use of this melody was attended with consequences of which he never dreamed, the practice of solmisation by "hexachords," or scales of six sounds only; (a practice, only abandoned in this century,) which consists in the adoption for each successive note of the hexachord of a set of names which are universally understood and extensively used to this day.

The first syllable of each verse (of Fig. 5) has been adopted as the name of the note above it:—*Ut* (for which *Do* is now substituted) for the first note of the first verse, *Re* for that of the second; and so on to *La*. *Si*, a modern addition, completes the modern septenary.

Guido makes no mention in any of his works either of the hexachord or of the solfa syllables. The use of the latter, however, may well be regarded as among those good indirect results which flow from all honest work, and which all honest work will eventually ensure, though when or how we know not.

I have more than once spoken of the music of these early times, as it may have seemed, disparagingly; and, as respects such attempts at harmony as those which you have heard, I could hardly have done otherwise. But I am far from wishing to disparage even very early Mediæval melody. I am going to try to get you to agree with me in liking it, though without very much hope that I shall succeed, so far at least as Ecclesiastical melody is concerned; for the secular melody of these times does not present the same difficulty. Let me explain.

In the Middle Ages, as in our own time, there were two kinds of music, sacred and secular; but the difference between them was then much more strongly marked than it is now.

Nearly all our music, sacred or secular, is in one respect alike; it is "in time." It is mensurable, or measurable music, *cantus mensurabilis* as the old writers called it; made up of, and divisible into, certain short successions of sounds or phrases of proportioned lengths. Our musical intelligence is unable to appreciate, as are our musical memories to retain, any succession of sounds that is not "in time." For instance, no modern musician could remember this from once hearing it.

Fig. 6.

You do not even recognise it. Let me play it in time.

Fig. 7.

Almost any modern melody, treated in this manner, might be made unrecognisable, even by its own composer. But there existed in the Middle Ages a species of melody which was absolutely *timeless;* and, up to a somewhat late period, no other was heard or practised in the Church. Of such melody a great deal has come down to us, in the service books of the Latin Church; and the attention of every traveller who has ever entered a Continental church must often have been called to certain strains, coarsely uttered perhaps; strange, dull, uncouth sort of stuff, if you will; but which, being altogether unlike anything ever heard outside the church walls, does, in spite of ourselves and in spite of the way in which it is often performed, force itself on our attention and extort a kind of respect. Of such melody, I repeat, a great deal has come down to us, on paper, or rather, parchment; but it seems to be admitted, among those who have studied it most closely, that the performance of it is a lost art. Great efforts have been made of late years, especially in France, to recover this; but they have not been attended with much success. The very existence of such melody would seem to be incompatible with that of the *cantus*

mensurabilis. In superseding mediæval sculpture, the printing-press, it has been said, destroyed it; in rendering it impracticable, the time-table destroyed mediæval "plain-song." I am unwilling however to dismiss this art without doing what I can to make you understand in what it consisted; and no amount of description will quite do this. I will, therefore, with your permission, try to convey my own idea of it by singing a strophe of a hymn known as the *Prose of Montpellier*, a MS. of which, of the tenth century, and therefore in *neuma* notation, was not long since brought to light by a French antiquary. I take also the opportunity of bringing a specimen of this notation, together with a translation of it before you. From a literary point of view, this "prose" is very interesting. It is one of many similar compositions, due to the almost universal belief which prevailed up to the expiration of the tenth century that the end of the world was imminent. Some of the finest thoughts and expressions in these have found a place in the magnificent hymn *Dies Iræ*, which forms so large a part of the Requiem or Mass for the Dead; which hymn, it now appears, is not an original composition, but a collection of fragments, the product of many hands and the growth of many centuries.

PROSE OF MONTPELLIER.

FROM A MS. OF THE TENTH CENTURY.

Translation.

Fig. 8.

PROSE OF MONTPELLIER.

FROM A MS. OF THE TENTH CENTURY.

Facsimile.

Fig. 9.

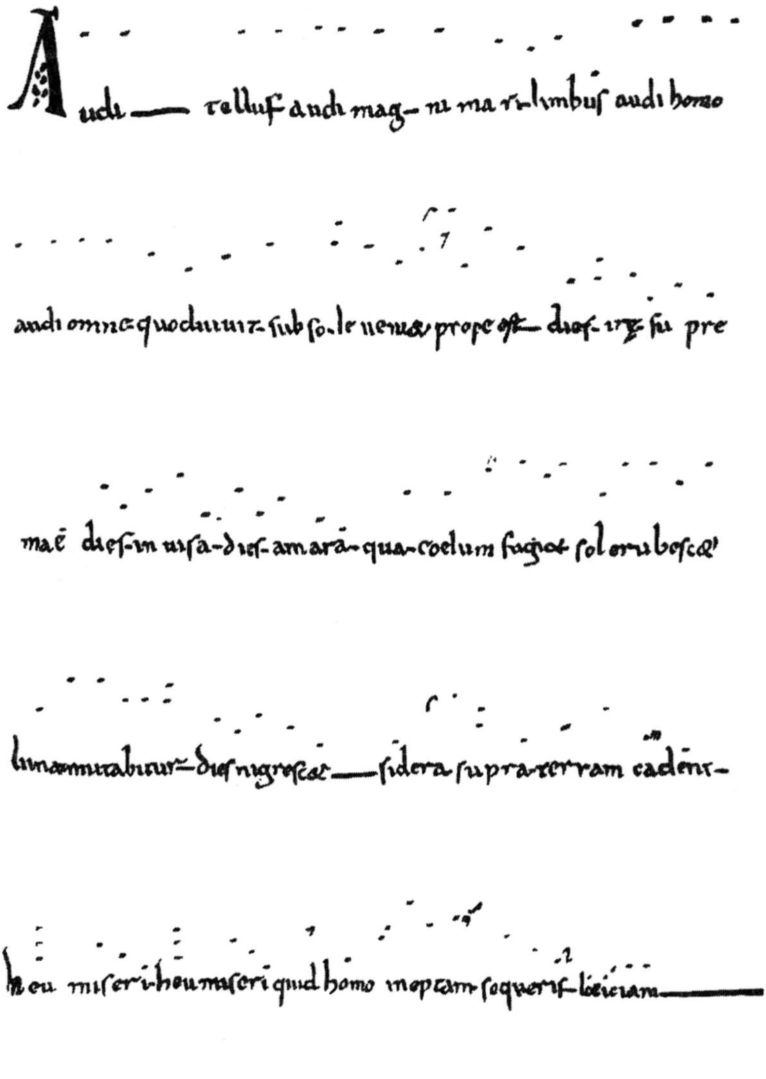

Up to a comparatively recent period many musical historians would seem to have laboured under the impression that this kind of music was the only music of the Middle Ages; that not only the rude people found expression for their passions and feelings, but that even the skilled Troubadour and Trouvère sang of war and of love, in strains as grim and as vague as that which you have just heard;—in fact, that *time* and the time-*table*, if not synonymous terms, are contemporaneous discoveries; and that our tonality had no existence till that existence was acknowledged by the theorists of modern times. It is true that, anterior to the eleventh century, there is no mention, by a scientific writer, of time or even of secular music; but, not to say that theory is the result, not the cause, of practice, and that art is always ahead of science, it seems as unreasonable to assume the existence of a period when all music was without time, as of a period when men did not walk or talk. Not to speak of the indisputable antiquity of the practice of *dancing*, inevitably accompanied by music, which, as inevitably, must have been mensurable music, recent research has thrown up a considerable number of melodies which, allowing the attempts to decipher them to have been even partially successful, certainly differ in their character from any ecclesiastical music of the same date. It might be added that a body of what is called "national melody" exists in every country, much of which is undoubtedly of great antiquity. How much of this however has undergone transformation in its passage from mouth to mouth, and from hand to hand, across such vast tracts of time, it is very hard to say. No nation is richer in this traditional music than our own, and I need not do more than refer you to the valuable and interesting work of Mr. Chappell,* for specimens of it alike numerous and interesting.

But what is written remains; unintelligible, misinterpreted

* "Popular Music of the Older Time." London, 1855–59.

perhaps, for a time; but always at hand for study and interrogation, and sooner or later enabled to tell its own story. A MS. of the ninth century is more trustworthy than a tradition of the nineteenth; and, as I have said, such MSS. exist, and we have at least begun to read them approximately. In the Bibliothèque Impériale of Paris* is one of this date (the ninth century) which contains eighteen Latin pieces accompanied by musical notation. Five of them are historical songs, eleven are on religious subjects, and two are odes of Boethius. Of the tenth century have recently been discovered a song relating to Otho III. Emperor of Germany, a convivial song, of which two tenth-century MSS. have been found, and two odes of Horace. Of somewhat later date, as might be expected, musical monuments become more plentiful, and, it may be added, more easy to interpret. A considerable number of these have been lately made known in various Continental periodical and other publications; in the "Annales Archéologiques," edited by M. Didron, in the "Revue Musicale," in the "Revue de la Musique Religieuse," and other periodicals. But by far the most interesting collection is to be found in M. de Coussemaker's "Histoire de l'Harmonie au Moyen Age," of which I have already spoken.

M. de Coussemaker does not ask his readers blindly to accept his interpretations of these MSS.; indeed he is anything but dogmatical about them. He presents us in every instance with facsimiles traced from the originals, to which he appends translations into modern notation. Of these translations three are before you. I must refer you to M. de Coussemaker's own work for a sight of the facsimiles, the fidelity of which I have myself tested by comparison with the originals in the Bibliothèque Impériale. The words of No. 10 relate to a very warlike ecclesiastic, a natural son of the Emperor Charlemagne, who perished in battle in the year 844.

* No. 1154.

LAMENT FOR THE ABBÉ HUG.

FROM A MS. OF THE NINTH CENTURY.

Fig. 10.

The words of No. 11 are of a very different character. They are part of an invitation to dinner to a friend: the friend being, you will observe, addressed as amic*a*, not amic*e*.

SONG.

FROM A MS. OF THE TENTH CENTURY.

Fig. 11.

The third of these specimens is from a MS. of the thirteenth century in the public library at Lille. The notation is comparatively modern, and the correctness of its interpretation admits of no doubt. The superscription describes it as a dance-tune, known in connexion with a *Trouvère* lay: "Cantilena de chorea super illam quæ incipit:" "*Qui grieve ma cointise se jou lai ce me font amouretes cau cuer ai.*" You will, I hope, agree with me in thinking it very pretty.

DANCE TUNE.

FROM A MS. OF THE THIRTEENTH CENTURY.

Fig. 12.

The original notation of the first two of these specimens is not only wanting in exactness as respects the *pitch* of the sounds to be represented, but it is altogether defective in another respect; it has no means of expressing their *lengths.* In vocal melody these characters would be measured chiefly by the accent and quantity of the syllables under them, which would be equally a guide in the barbarous *diaphony* or *organum* of which you have had examples; as also in *faux-bourdon,* an improved kind of diaphony. But within fifty years of the death of Guido (at about the end of the eleventh century) a new form of musical art made its appearance, the characteristic of which was the combination of sounds of unequal lengths; music in which two or more sounds succeeded one another, while one, equal to them in length, was sustained. This was called *discantus* or (*Anglicè*) "descant." Descant, it is plain, would argue the existence of some system of musical proportion among sounds of different duration, and *written* descant, some means of distinguishing such sounds from one another. As might be expected, we hear of both inventions at about the same epoch, the middle of the twelfth century, when the first treatise on the *Cantus Mensurabilis,* by Franco of Cologne, was made known, when *notes* appear first to have been used, and signs to represent the raising or depressing of individual sounds (*sharps and flats*) first came into being.

The epoch of Franco of Cologne has been the subject of much controversy; some writers placing him in the second half of the eleventh century, some in the second half of the twelfth, and some at the beginning of the thirteenth. Indeed an attempt has been made to solve the problem by the supposition that there were two writers of the same name. Be this as it may, musical notation must have made many improvements by the end of the eleventh century; for the first known specimen of descant is of this date. There is a facsimile of it in

M. de Coussemaker's book. The original is in the Bibliothèque Impériale of Paris.* The musical characters are "transitional neumas"—almost notes.

The last years of the twelfth, and the first of the thirteenth, centuries must be regarded as forming one of the most interesting epochs in the history of civilization. It is the epoch of the second, third, fourth, and fifth crusades, and of the apogee of papal power and monastic influence; of the invention, though not yet the recognition, of the pointed arch; of the poet-musicians of Provence, Northern France, and Belgium—the Troubadours and Trouvères; and, in the matter with which we are at present most concerned, of the adoption of musical notes, the time-table, and descant; the materials and the elements of, perhaps, the firstborn among the arts, but, as it has proved, the last of them to attain maturity.

Among all of these and other circumstances of this epoch it would not be difficult to trace a connexion. The fine arts, in their greatest force and in their highest perfection, are but the expression of the condition of the world in which they are practised. In music, the mechanical diaphony or organum, and in architecture, the equally mechanical semicircular arch of the early Middle Ages, present themselves as types of monasticism — of its timidity, its narrowness, and the monotony of its average existence; while descant, like the pointed arch, with which, I repeat, it exactly synchronizes, may be regarded as the type of active life—with all its dangers, its difficulties, and its possibilities of failure; but with what it is worth braving all these to enjoy—its freedom.

At this epoch the work of the first period of musical history was really achieved, and no second step so . reat as that from organum to descant was, for many long years, possible; and though the *new art* was practised, and to some extent developed, by the artists of the thirteenth and fourteenth centuries, no musical inventor or reformer to be compared with Ambrose, Gregory, Hucbald, Guido, or Franco appeared till the opening of the second period—the consideration of which we must defer till we meet again.

THE SECOND PERIOD.

FROM ABOUT A.D. 1400 TO ABOUT A.D. 1600.

MUSICAL SCIENCE IN THE TWELFTH CENTURY — FAUX-BOURDON AND EXTEMPORANEOUS DESCANT—ADAM DE LA HALE—THE FOURTEENTH CENTURY—COUNTERPOINT—JEAN DE MURIS—GUILLAUME DE MACHAULT—THE ORGAN—LANDINO—SECULAR MUSIC—ITS INFLUENCE ON ECCLESIASTICAL—BELGIAN EXPERIMENTS IN COUNTER-POINT—BELGIAN MUSICIANS IN ROME—DUFAY—CANON AND IMITATION—THE "NEW" BELGIAN SCHOOL—OCKENHEIM—JOSQUIN DEPRÈS—HIS CONTEMPORARIES AND PUPILS—THE PUBLICATIONS OF PETRUCCI—MUSIC IN ROME AT THE BEGINNING OF THE SIXTEENTH CENTURY—THE ORATORIO—FILIPPO NERI AND GIOVANNI ANIMUCCIA—CLAUDE GOUDIMEL—PALESTRINA—CHURCH MUSIC BEFORE PALESTRINA—THE "MISSA PAPÆ MARCELLI"—ROLAND DE LATTRE—THE MADRIGAL—EXTENSIVE CULTIVATION OF MUSIC AT THE END OF THE SIXTEENTH CENTURY—LUCA MARENZIO—ENGLISH COMPOSERS OF THE SECOND PERIOD.

THE SECOND PERIOD.

At our last meeting we were occupied with a very rapid, and of necessity slight, survey of the progress of music from the end of the fourth to that of the fourteenth century. After about eight hundred of these thousand years, *i.e.*, in the twelfth century, we find the elements of what we now call music, and the apparatus without which it would have been impossible to turn them to account, at the service of the musician. Descant, though of a somewhat rude kind, was extensively practised; the two principles on which our modern notation is based, that the place of a note determines its pitch, and the shape its length, were recognised; and means were presented, in the flat and the sharp, of expressing every recognised variety of musical intonation. Much of this apparatus was too delicate for any hands into which, at this time, it could possibly have fallen; the majority of musicians did not at first attempt to avail themselves of it. Diaphony, the accompaniment of plain-song with consecutive octaves, fifths, and fourths, had died out in most places; but faux-bourdon, a somewhat improved variety of it, and extemporaneous descant were the nearest approaches to music made, even in the Pope's Chapel, by the best singers, up to the time of the return of the Papal Court to Rome, in the year 1377. Avignon, however, must then have fallen as much behind its age, in the matter of music, as Rome subsequently got ahead of it. In the first part of the thirteenth century the *Déchanteurs*, or harmonizers, were a separate class, who put into form the musical ideas of others; but later in the century we hear of a *Trouvère* who was not only, as a matter of course, a poet and a melodist, but a harmonist also. This was Adam de la Hale, born in 1240, and surnamed "Le Bossu d'Arras." Some three-part songs of his were, some years since, discovered and interpreted by the eminent French critic M. Fétis. The originals are in the Bibliothèque Impériale. The structure of these songs, though still rude, is in advance of that of any known preceding or contemporaneous music. Adam de la Hale however has a claim on our notice much stronger than he would owe to these detached pieces. He is the composer, so far as has yet been ascertained, of the first comic opera. It is entitled "Li Gieus [le jeu] de Robin et de Marion," the same Robin Hood and the same Maid Marian who have been the subjects of so much poetical and plastic illustration among ourselves. The Bibliothèque Impériale contains two contemporary MSS. of this work, one perfect, the other incomplete; the music never having been filled into the spaces left for it in the latter by the copyist of the words. These MSS. I have carefully examined. You will find a perfect transcript of the *libretto* only in the "Théâtre Français au Moyen Age"* of Messrs. Monmerqué and Michel; and the Société des Bibliophiles, of Paris, had a facsimile of the complete MS. made in 1822, of which they printed only twenty-five copies. M. Fétis, also, has illustrated an article in an early number of the "Revue Musicale" with a specimen as well of this opera as of De la Hale's three-part songs. They are before you.

The trio (Fig. 13) is deserving of careful study. Traces of the barbarous diaphony, from which this composer was probably one of the first to try and emancipate himself, strike the eye and the ear more than once. The consecutive octaves and fifths are however found chiefly between the end of one phrase and the beginning of another; and some ingenuity is shown in

* Paris. 1839.

concealing them where this is not the case, as in the progression from the second to the third bar. The tonality, to a modern ear, is, both at the beginning and at the end, equivocal; but the modulations, first into G and then into F, are orderly and elegant. One or two modifications would make this little piece unexceptionable.

PART SONG, BY ADAM DE LA HALE.

FROM A MS. OF THE THIRTEENTH CENTURY.

Fig. 13.

The melody (Fig. 14) from " Li Gieus de Robin et de Marion" demands no apology; it is an exceedingly pretty one. I present it as it is in the original MS., only substituting crotchets and quavers for longs and breves, and marking the bars. With the addition of a slight and simple accompaniment, this song is still able to give pleasure. It belongs to the part of Robin, and should therefore be sung by a man's voice. There is a second verse, separated from it in the opera by a few words of dialogue.

SONG, FROM ADAM DE LA HALE'S *ROBIN ET MARION.*

FROM A MS. OF THE THIRTEENTH CENTURY.

Fig. 14.

The beginning of the next century (the fourteenth) furnishes us with a remarkable evidence of musical advancement in the word *contrapunctum* or (*Anglicè*), "counterpoint,"—*i.e.*, point against point, or, as we should now say, note against note. This word was first used in lieu of the word descant, in the writings of Jean de Muris, the greatest musical theorist of the fourteenth century. Its appearance in many treatises extensively circulated in this author's time, shows that points, or musical notes, were then pretty generally accepted as the symbols of musical sounds. The middle of the century gives us the first example of music of four parts, in a Mass performed at the coronation of Charles V. of France (in 1360), and composed by Guillaume de Machault, better, and more deservedly, known as one of the earliest French Poets. As a musician, Guillaume de Machault cannot be accepted as a type even of the remote period in which he lived.

The organ must have reached some degree of mechanical perfection in this century, for we find a certain Francesco Landino, a Florentine, sometimes described as Francesco dei Organi, and sometimes as Francesco Cieco (for he was blind), distinguishing himself greatly in the fêtes given by the Republic of Venice in honour of the King of Cyprus, in the year 1364. Landino attained considerable reputation also as a composer, and some part songs recently brought to light, like those of Adam de la Hale through the diligence of French archæologists, show that this reputation was not undeserved.

The musical historians of the last century—our own Burney and Hawkins not excepted—would seem, one and all, to have sat down to write under the influence of two hypotheses, both quite consistent with the preposterous views of mediæval life and mediæval art common among their contemporaries:—(1), that before the fifteenth century, if so soon, secular music had no existence; and (2), as would necessarily follow, that the history of all modern music must be traced in that of Church music. Recent research has shown, on the contrary,—(1), that there has always been a music differing as widely in character as in purpose from Church music; and (2), that this secular music, till lately so strangely ignored, is the veritable *fons et origo* of all that is most worthy of admiration in the Church music of the Second Period. Of this secular music, it is true, we as yet know but little. Few specimens of it have been recovered, and to many of these the key has not yet been found. The subject moreover is a new one, and there has not yet been time for sufficiently extensive research or careful investigation in respect to it. What has been done already, however, justifies the hope that, sooner or later, we shall recover some knowledge of the music of the thirteenth and fourteenth centuries;—the music of the latest and greatest among the Troubadours and Trouvères; the music of the Gardens of Boccaccio; the music to which Dante might have listened as "his Casella" sang; the music which gave occupation to a chorus and orchestra when Petrarch received the laurel crown in the Roman Capitol; the music of the Squire, the Miller, the Pardonour, the Sumptnour and the Host of Chaucer;—in fact, the music of that particular portion of the "dark ages" to which the world is indebted for Notre Dame de Chartres and Westminster Abbey; for the sculptures at Rheims, the painted windows at Bourges, the metalwork at Aix-la-Chapelle, the frescoes at Padua; for the sonnets of Petrarch, the tales of Boccaccio, the Canterbury Pilgrimage, and the Divine Comedy.

The fourteenth century, it will be remembered, was the great epoch of Belgian prosperity. Antwerp, Ghent, Ypres, Bruges, Louvain, and other cities still exhibit evidences of their former splendour; not so much in their ecclesiastical buildings, not for a moment to be compared with those of France and the North of Italy, as in examples of municipal and domestic architecture more numerous and more splendid than could be furnished by all the rest of Northern Europe combined. In these beautiful towns, secure at least from the worst of those evils which oppressed most other Continental nations, the Art, one of whose best privileges it is to gladden and to beautify domestic life, was much practised; and many of those grand contrapuntal effects which afterwards became such essential features in Church music that they seem now out of place elsewhere were first essayed, not in monastic or metropolitan choirs, but in the back-parlours of Flemish shopkeepers.

In the domestic music of the Flemings of the fourteenth century musical Art and musical science first worked together to a common end. For centuries past scholars without number had expounded, with more or less clearness, and no result, the divisions of the monochord; the three genera; the modes Dorian, Phrygian, Lydian, Mæso-lydian; the hexachords, natural, hard, and soft; and whatever else might constitute the science of music in those days,—the body of fact and speculation which gave it a place in the "quadrivium;" a body of fact and of speculation having about as much relation to practical music as it had to comparative anatomy. On the other hand, the singers and players had gone on, alike indifferent to, and ignorant of, "all this learning," trusting to their instincts, accepting a combination here, rejecting it there, and actually building up, bit by bit, that new art which was afterwards to furnish material for a science not only new but, it may be hoped, true. That this union of theory and practice was first brought about in the Netherlands is certain. That some of the earliest results of it handed down to us should be in the form of Church music is, of course, consistent with the spirit of the age in which it was produced.

It has recently been ascertained from the records of the Pope's Chapel, that several Belgian musicians visited Rome in the last years of the fourteenth century, bringing with them, along with other music, the first Masses that had ever been seen there in written counterpoint. I have already stated that in the Pope's Chapel at Avignon, the service was then still sung in faux-bourdon, an improved "diaphony," and in extemporaneous descant.

In the list of these Belgians is found the name of William Dufay, who was certainly a singer in the Pontifical Chapel in 1380; *i.e.*, three years after the return of the Popes from Avignon to Rome. Few particulars have come down to us respecting this musician. He was born at Chimay, in Hainault, about the year 1350, and died at Rome in 1432. All else that is known about him is that he had a tenor voice, and that he visited the court of the Dukes of Burgundy at Dijon; for an old French writer, Martin le Franc, in a Poem called "Le Champion des Dames," speaks of Dufay and a contemporary, Binchois, as having betrayed something like jealousy at the performance of some blind musicians there.

J'ai vu Binchois avoir vergogne
Et soy taire emprez leur rebelle,*
Et du Fay despité et frongne
Qu'il n'a melodie si belle.

In the absence of fact one may be pardoned a little speculation. I should gather from these verses that the writer took the popular and poetical, in contradistinction to the scholastic, view of music; and that there were in the fourteenth century, as in the nineteenth, people with a pardonable weakness for melody or tune, and very indifferent to music which was wanting in it. I am unacquainted with the secular music of Dufay; but if it bore any resemblance to his sacred music, it must have had a hard battle to fight against the sprightly strains of a party of blind fiddlers. The compositions of Dufay which I have seen are of a grave, grandiose character, harsh in places to a modern ear, but incomparably superior in design and clearness of texture to the mass of Guillaume de Machault which has been already mentioned.

Dufay, Binchois, and their contemporaries, who were numerous, may be said to be recent discoveries; for their very names, not to say their works, have lain for ages hidden under those of a later generation—the masters of "the *new* Belgian school"—Ockenheim, his contemporaries and pupils. Their relations to their predecessors add another to the many proofs furnished by the history of literature, art, and science, that behind every great man, or set of great men, is hidden another great man, or another set of great men, who have filled for them the indispensable, but, alas! ungrateful, office of pioneer. One of the most valuable resources of musical science is "canon." Canon, I need hardly say, means simply rule; and musicians have at different epochs subjected themselves to rules many of which are doubtless pedantic and absurd enough. But that particular kind of canon which consists in the imitation at a short interval

* Rebec.

of time of one "part" by another has long been, and probably always will be, a characteristic feature of every sustained musical composition of high class. For musical composition does not consist in an unintermittent presentation of new thoughts, but in the development, the pursuit to their ultimate consequences, of a few thoughts, sometimes even of a single one; technically, in making the same passage heard successively in various scales, in various parts, and under various forms of accompaniment. The art of "canon," heretofore traced only to the "new" Belgian school of Ockenheim, was, it now appears, practised half a century earlier by Dufay; and the earliest specimen of it yet discovered is by him. There are two very good examples of canon in an extant *Benedictus* by Dufay. I will play it, begging you to remember,—first, that it is written for two voices, not for an instrument; secondly, that it is five hundred years old; and thirdly (once for all), that this is not a concert. Some of you will recognise a resemblance in the opening of this canon to that of a very pretty part song by an English composer of the sixteenth century which has been recently revived, "In going to my lonely bed." I have never seen an original or contemporary copy of this movement. I take mine (at second hand) from the appendix to Kiesewetter's "History of the Modern Music of Western Europe." The notation is modernized, but the proportions of the notes are of course the same as in the original. (Fig. 15.)

BENEDICTUS, BY GUILLAUME DUFAY

Fig. 15.

Ockenheim, though not the inventor of imitation, doubtless improved it greatly. He is however less interesting to us as a composer than as a teacher. His best works were his pupils, and among these was the musician with whose name the last years of the fifteenth and the first of the sixteenth century are commonly associated in musical history, Josquin Deprès.

Music, it is often said, is the only language which has any claim to be called universal; and, by parity of reason, its professors should be regarded as the only real citizens of the world. It would be hard to find an instance of a celebrated person of any other class whose native country has ever been matter of uncertainty or dispute. We hear, it is true, of more than one city which has claimed to be the birthplace of a Homer or a Livy; but there is no question as to the former—assuming his individual existence—having been a Greek, and the latter, an Italian. The musicians of the fourteenth, fifteenth, and even sixteenth centuries seem to have been looked upon as common property; for they have been appropriated, or at least claimed, by every people at all covetous of distinction in the Fine Arts.

Josquin Deprès, the glory of the Belgian school of music, is of course considered by the Belgians as a compatriot. In virtue of his name having been Italianized into *Del Prato*, he has been occasionally added to the long list of illustrious Italians; a birthplace even, Prato in Tuscany, having been invented for him. An eminent German historian speaks of him as a countryman, on the ground that the Low Countries are, ethnologically and geographically, a part of Germany; and the French lay claim to him, in virtue of the fact that a portion of these countries was added to France, about two centuries after Josquin's death, by Louis XIV. Nor has the year of his birth been matter of less dispute than the place of it. It is even uncertain whether he studied in Paris or at Tours, where his instructor, Ockenheim, was some time resident as Treasurer of St. Martin's and Choir Master to Louis XI. On the other hand, it has been ascertained that he was a choir-boy in the cathedral church of St. Quintin, in Belgic Gaul, or French Flanders; and it is therefore probable that he was born in or near that city. It is certain too that he had been "for some time" a singer in the Pope's chapel, in the year 1484, when he could hardly have been less than five-and-twenty years of age. He must have been born, therefore, before 1460.

Josquin's visit to Rome, made during the pontificate of Sixtus IV., is, as respects its results, one of the most important events recorded in the history of music.

You will have noticed that during the First Period the scene of our narrative was almost exclusively Italy, and where not, the South of France; but that the work of the Second Period has been carried on, so far, in the North of Europe; indeed in a comparatively small district where, from causes already stated, the Arts had found a more secure asylum than in any other part of the Continent. Though there is reason to believe and to know that music, especially secular music, was much practised in Italy during the fifteenth and even the fourteenth centuries, the Italians had not begun to cultivate, indeed were hardly cognizant of the existence of, those higher branches of the art which were already so flourishing in the Low Countries. While in the North of Europe excellent schools of composition and practical music were to be found, in Italy there was nothing worthy of the name; and while, in the churches of Belgium and France, native music not altogether unworthy of the structures in which it might be heard, was produced in abundance, the only exceptions to the miserable faux-bourdon and extemporaneous descant known to the Italian churches were works of foreigners. The Church music of Dufay and his contemporaries had about the end of the preceding (the fourteenth) century found its way to Rome, and some Gallo-Belgian musicians had subsequently found their way thither also. But their stay was evidently too short to be productive of any permanent effect.

Even Josquin did not make a long sojourn in Italy. After but a few years' residence, he quitted Rome, on the death of his patron Sixtus IV. (in 1484) and presented himself at the court of Hercules I., Duke of Ferrara. There is no reason for believing that he met with any other than the hospitable reception generally afforded by this accomplished and munificent Prince to men of genius of all kinds, for Josquin's reputation was by this time European. Some accident, however, or more likely an inconstant temper, took him soon back again to the north; after which we find him resident at Paris, at the court of Louis XII.

A personal service which he rendered his new master has been recorded, among other examples of the versatility of Josquin's talent. The king, though fond of music, had never studied it. Not only so, his natural aptitude for the art was of the very least. In plain terms, his Majesty had a very bad voice, and sang habitually out of tune. Fortunately for those of his subjects whose privilege it was to be immediately about him, he was quite aware of his own infirmity. One day however the whim seized him to commission Josquin to write something in which he himself could take part. Josquin met the difficulty in a very ingenious manner. He constructed a quartet, the two upper parts of which formed a canon in unison, to which he added a free bass; the fourth part, the *vox regis*, as he somewhat saucily called it, being confined to a single note, which it was the business of the king to reiterate, almost incessantly, throughout the piece.

Josquin was a man of wit. Many instances are recorded of his ready exercise of it. His office at court, however honourable, was evidently not a very remunerative one; for he is said to have been reduced to indigence while waiting for a small benefice that had been promised him by his royal master. In his distress he applied to a courtier whom he had formerly known in Italy, who always replied to him in the same words;

"Lascia fare mi," "leave the matter to me." Weary of this reply, he composed a mass, of which the principal subject consisted of the notes *La, Sol, Fa, Re, Mi;* which notes, *and syllables,* repeated over and over again in a long work, immediately excited attention, and eventually brought the matter again to the king's mind; to so little purpose, however, that Josquin had to resort to a new contrivance. He set as an anthem for the Chapel Royal the words "Memor esto verbi tuo," "O think upon Thy servant as concerning Thy word;" which being still without effect, he then tried his hand upon "Portio mea non est in terrâ vivantium." This was irresistible: Josquin obtained his benefice and poured out his gratitude in a third anthem, "Bonitatem fecisti cum servo tuo, Domine," "Lord, Thou hast dealt graciously with Thy servant." A cynical French Biographer tells us that this third composition was not at all up to the mark of its predecessors. Let us hope this is not true.

I cannot afford to dwell longer on the *personnel* of Josquin Deprès whose career might well furnish material for an entire lecture. He is said, later in life, to have taken service with the Emperor Maximilian who eventually gave him a canonry at Condé where he ended his days, about the year 1515.

But for considerations which I shall have to bring under your notice in my next Lecture, one might be inclined to despair of the possibility of lasting fame for any musical composer or composition. During the lifetime of Josquin Deprès, his popularity at least equalled that of any musician who has yet appeared. The Abbate Baini, to whom I shall again have occasion to refer, and who has left a splendid testimony of his admiration for the music of the Second Period in his "Life of Palestrina,"* speaks thus of Josquin:—

* "Memorie Storico-critiche della Vita di G. P. da Palestrina," &c. &c. Compilate da Giuseppe Baini, Sacerdote Romano, Cappellano Cantore, e Direttore della Cappella Pontificia. Roma, 1828. Vol. ii. p. 407.

"In a short time, by his new productions, he becomes the idol of Europe. There is no longer tolerance for any one but Josquin. Nothing is beautiful unless it be the work of Josquin. Josquin alone is sung in every chapel in Christendom. Nobody but Josquin in Italy, nobody but Josquin in France, nobody but Josquin in Germany, in Flanders, in Hungary, in Spain—Josquin and Josquin alone."

The praises of his contemporaries might fill a small volume. Luther, in musical matters an excellent authority, a singer and composer, said of him, "Other musicians do what they can with notes, Josquin does what he likes with them." His death was followed by innumerable elegies, epitaphs, and other encomiastic pieces, many of which were set to music by his pupils. Among his works are found compositions of every variety practised in his day. Greatest and most prolific in the greatest style, he was no less delightful, to *his* public at least, in compositions of a lighter class. He was not simply more learned in the science, and more skilled in the art, of music than any predecessor or contemporary; he was unquestionably a great and original genius. I shall have occasion to speak of him in another lecture as having discovered and appreciated certain musical resources which cannot be said to have been fully turned to account till at least a century after his death.

And with all this, what living singer has ever sung, or what living amateur has ever heard, a note of his music? Specimens of it are not current, it is true; but neither are they inaccessible. Three hundred and fifty years are as nothing in the lifetime of a book, a building, a statue,—even of a picture, so much more perishable. To speak only of our own era. Dante had need of a commentator before Josquin could have learnt to read; the frescoes of Giotto were beginning to decay ere he visited Italy, and the beautiful cathedral of St. Quintin had entered its third century ere he first raised his voice in it. Has the interest in these persons and things declined? Moments there have been, doubtless, when it has been less extensive and less hearty than it is now; but they have known no lengthened term of neglect or indifference. Not so the old music and the old musicians. "The cold chain of silence" has hung over the harp of Josquin Deprès for three centuries. Hidden first by his immediate successors, and subsequently, like them in turn, by theirs—all as much his works as were his masses and motets—his productions can scarcely be said to have survived him, save in those of other men. It is to be feared that this indifference, if not to Josquin's memory, at least to his music, will prove irremediable: his fame will know "no second spring."

I have said that Josquin's visit to Rome was an event of the greatest importance as regards the history of music. It was the signal for a new invasion of the Italian peninsula. Again, after an interval of near a thousand years, were the Goth and the Burgundian, the Belgian and the Gaul to set foot on Italian soil; but this time with what different intent! and in what a different capacity! Not to obliterate or to deface, but to restore and to edify; not as barbarian conquerors, but as teachers of the gentlest and the humanest of the arts.

This new immigration of "barbarians" was a great step in political economy. It established free-trade in that which only one small people had to sell, and all the rest of the world wanted to buy. In the latter part of the fifteenth century the musical science and skill which had hitherto been pent up within the confines of the Low Countries, were distributed all over Europe. At this epoch we find the contemporaries and pupils of Josquin in every court and great city of the Continent. Tinctor, Garnier, and Hycart (all three Gallo-Belgians) were laying the foundations of a school at Naples, destined afterwards to take precedence, for a time, of all others. Of Josquin's pupils, and countrymen, Nicholas Gombert was chapel-master to the Emperor Charles V. John Mouton held the same office at the court of Francis I. Eleazer Genet, surnamed *Carpentras*, from the place of his birth, made so great an impression on Pope Leo X., by his setting of a portion of the "Lamentations of Jeremiah," that he made him a bishop (*in partibus*), and afterwards sent him on a special mission into France as legate. Henry Isaac, a German by birth but a Belgian by education, was at Florence composing masses for the church of St. Giovanni, and Carnival Songs for Lorenzo de' Medici; and, a little later, after long years of wanderings, even into Hungary and Bohemia, we find Andrew Willaert (another Fleming) settled, as it proved, for life in Venice; there to found another school whose disciples were afterwards to carry back to the north, with large interest, the capital advanced by her children—northern strength graced by southern sweetness.

It would be useless to multiply these instances. One proof of Belgian influence at this time, however, must be cited. About the year 1502,* Ottavio Petrucci, a native of Fossembrone in the Papal States, who had recently invented musical types, set up a printing press in Venice, from which he sent forth in rapid succession, during a series of years, a prodigious number of Masses, Motets, and other music by the most eminent masters of the time. These, with hardly an exception, were all compositions of the Gallo-Belgian school. If it be considered that the printer was himself neither a Belgian nor a Frenchman, and that he printed, of course, such works as he thought would find the best sale, we have irrefragable evidence of the popularity of Gallo-Belgian music at this epoch.

But it is to Rome that we must now turn all our attention; for it is in the Eternal City that the somewhat tangled web of our history has to be taken up, and for a time kept in hand.

Notwithstanding the number of Belgian masters who visited and taught in Italy in the last years of the fifteenth and the first of the sixteenth century, no regular music school was opened in Rome before the year 1540. Many Italians how-

* Only half a century after the invention of printing.

ever had already profited, directly or indirectly, by Belgian instruction and example. Constanzo Festa, at the time of his death, (in 1545) had attained a great reputation as a composer in the highest departments of his art. He was one of the creators of the "Madrigal:" and a *Te Deum* of his has been sung on the election of every new Pope since his time; *i.e.*, for more than three hundred years, in the course of which the Roman See has had no less than thirty-three occupants.

The two brothers Giovanni and Paulo Animuccia, Florentines by birth but Romans in training and residence, had also attained great reputation at this time. The name of the former has come down to us chiefly through his subsequent connexion with San Filippo Neri; since to this connexion may be traced the origin of the "Oratorio," that noblest form of musical art which, strangely enough, seeing its origin, owes its development almost exclusively to Protestant genius. Crescembini* tells us:—

"The Oratorio, a poetical composition formerly a commixture of the dramatic and narrative styles, but now entirely a musical drama, had its origin from San Filippo Neri, who, in his chapel, after sermons and other devotions, in order to allure young people to pious offices, and to detain them from earthly pleasures, had hymns, psalms, and such like prayers sung by one or more voices." "Among these spiritual songs were dialogues; and these entertainments, becoming more frequent and improving every year, were the occasion that, in the seventeenth century, *Oratorios* were invented, so called from their origin."†

The society formed by Filippo (in 1540) was called "La Congregazione dei Padri dell' Oratorio;" from *orare*, to pray. The form of composition, therefore, takes its name eventually from the pious exercise which brought San Filippo and his disciples together; and immediately, from the place in which they were carried on.

* "Storia della Volgar Poesia," vol. i. bk. 1.
† Hawkins's "Musical History," vol. iii. p. 441.

The first Music School established in Rome was opened by Claude Goudimel, a native of Besançon, now in France. The year of his birth has not been precisely ascertained, but there is good reason for supposing it to have been 1510. It is certain that he was a person of considerable accomplishment, not merely in his own art. Some Latin letters, addressed by him to his friend Paul Melissus, are said to exhibit a pure and elegant style. Nothing however has come down to us about his training, or manner of life, previously to 1540, a little before which year he had made himself known in Rome. He resided in that city about fifteen years; subsequently to which we hear of him as partner in a musical printing-office in Paris, and afterwards as being engaged in the arrangement of music to the Metrical Psalms of Clement Marot and Theodore Beza, his connexion with whom led doubtless to his adoption of their opinions, and subsequently to his premature and violent death. He was one of the victims of the massacre of St. Bartholomew,—among the number of the Calvinists at Lyons who, on the 24th of August, 1572, were precipitated into the Rhone.*

The compositions of Goudimel, numerous and excellent, are chiefly ecclesiastical, and written before his change of religion. Among the subjects of his labours in secular part-music was a selection of the Odes of Horace. His arrangements of the metrical Psalms were never used, nor intended to be used, in public worship. He expressly dedicates them to private devotion. Indeed Calvin, unlike Luther, seems never to have recognised music as a means of religious expression, scarcely

* The biographer of Palestrina, Baini, apologizes for not occupying himself "degli elogi convenienti ad un uomo di tanto merito," as Goudimel, thus:—"Il fine tragico però cui andò quell' infelice *meritamente* soggetto in Lione nella sanguinosa giornata dei 24 Augusto del 1572, da poi che sconsigliato abbracciò nel suo ritorno in Francia il partito degli Ugonotti, e sfacciatamente mostronne l'attaccamento con porre in musica i salmi tradotti da Clemente Marot, e da Teodoro Beza mi obbliga a tirare un velo sopra la sua memoria."—"Memorie Storico-critiche della Vita, &c." vol. i. p. 27.

even to have appreciated it as an aid to devotion. The music of his followers has at any rate always been the most meagre and unlovely conceivable.

I could not have spared even these few moments to Claude Goudimel, albeit a good musician and an interesting character, but for a fact, yet to be mentioned, which has directed far more attention to his name than his works or even his melancholy death would ever of themselves have done.

Among his pupils, the majority of whom might have some claims to a less rapid notice than this, was the greatest composer the world had yet seen,—the "Princeps Musicæ," the type and glory of the Second Period, Palestrina.

Giovanni Pierluigi (*Anglicè*, John Peter-Lewis) was born at Palestrina, near Rome, in the year 1524. It is not known how, or from whom, he learnt the elements of music; but at the age of sixteen (in 1540) he entered the school recently opened in Rome by Claude Goudimel. In 1551 (ætat. 27) he was appointed master of the boys in the Capella Giulia, and Chapel-master of the Vatican Basilica. In 1554 he gave his first publication to the world; and Pope Julius III., to whom he dedicated it, signified his approbation of the contents by appointing the author one of the singers in the Pontifical Chapel. The next Pope, Marcellus II., unfortunately for Palestrina, lived only twenty days after his election; but his successor, the severe Paul IV., an uncompromising reformer in his own way, was on his accession shocked to find that of the singers in the Pontifical Chapel no less than three were married! Of these culprits Palestrina was one, and he was punished accordingly, by the loss of his office. He was not long however in finding another. Two months after his expulsion from the Pope's Chapel he was made Master of the Choir of St. John Lateran. He subsequently exchanged this office for a similar one in the Church of Santa Maria Maggiore, which he held from 1561 to 1571, the ten most prolific years of his life. On the death of Animuccia, in 1571 (Pius V. being Pope), he took office again in St. Peter's and, at the request of San Filippo Neri, in the Oratory. Besides this, he undertook the direction of a School of Composition which had been established by Gio. Mar. Nanino just before. A short time after this he was entrusted by Gregory XIII. with the revision of the Chants of the Gradual and the Roman Antiphonary. To assign a task of this kind to a man of genius is to try to cut blocks with a razor. Michael Angelo might as profitably have been employed as a quarry-man, or Raphael in the manufacture of paint-brushes. He left it unfinished, even at the end of twenty years. In 1580, Palestrina, then fifty-six years of age, lost his wife, "whom he had married young. and who had proved," says Baini, "sua fedele compagna" for more than thirty years. She was the mother of four sons, three of whom, after showing promise of almost hereditary genius, had died early. He survived her fourteen years. Palestrina died on the 2nd of February, 1594, aged seventy.

Palestrina presents himself to us under two aspects, relatively and positively,—relatively to his immediate predecessors and with every allowance for the state of the world at the epoch when his lot was cast in it; positively, in respect to those great canons to which all works of art, of whatever kind or time, must be subjected.

To understand his relative greatness it is necessary, of course, to understand what was the condition of his art when he began to practise it. Happily this need not take us long. A few words indeed might almost enable us to do it. Josquin Deprès, who had found musical science and musical art almost strangers to each other, made them acquainted; Palestrina made them one.

Although it is certain that, could many of the productions of the Gallo-Belgian school of the epoch of Josquin be presented with anything like the same means and appliances that are now so frequently brought to bear on music of epochs nearer to our own, all persons of cultivated taste would recognise in them high and always rare qualities,—dignity, continuity, and what is included under the somewhat vague term "breadth;" yet it is equally certain that these qualities were rather the result of calculation on the part of the musician than of sentiment; rather the necessary consequence of working out certain principles than the irrepressible expression of an artist's feeling. The grandeur of this music would seem to be that of the tubular bridge rather than of the pointed church; and our sensations on hearing it would probably be more nearly akin to those derived from working out a proposition of Euclid than from reading an act of Shakspeare or a canto of Dante. So little able were the composers of this epoch to trust to their own impulses, so little conscious were they of their own really great strength, that there is hardly an instance to be found among their works of a composition built on an original theme; the practice among them being universal of working on some fragment of known melody.

The cramping influence of this practice needs no demonstration, so far as art is concerned; and abuses, the existence of which nothing but the most overwhelming evidence would make credible, grew up in connexion with it which very nearly drove music out of the sanctuary and turned in another direction the broad and deep river of divine harmony which has since flowed on uninterruptedly through ten generations. So long as musicians confined themselves to fragments of ecclesiastical melody, as canvases on which to embroider the flowers of their musical rhetoric, the Church made no complaint; although, as we shall see, she had other grounds for dissatisfaction with their works. But from the very earliest periods of descant, ecclesiastical musicians had been in the habit of taking the secular melodies of the time, and working *them* into their ecclesiastical compositions. It was as though, in our day, a musician were to compose a *Te Deum* or *Magnificat* of which one of the parts should consist of "Gentle Troubadour," "The Power of Love," or any other current tune that struck his fancy. But this is as nothing to what really happened. Not satisfied with the tunes, they transported words and all bodily into their works; and a hundred MSS. exist to show that while the soprano, alto, and bass might be singing "Ad Te levavi oculos meos," or any other words of like character, the tenor, always the agent in this shameless violation of decency, might utter "Belle dame me prie de chanter," or perhaps something infinitely more impertinent.

Nor was even this all. The Church had great reason to complain of the treatment which the *text* of the Antiphonary and the Hymnal received at the hands of those who set it to music, and even of the music to which it was set; so far as its purpose, promoting the glory of God or stirring the affections of men, was concerned. The work of the head, not of the heart of the artist, it might engage the intellect, but could never quicken the pulses or call tears into the eyes of his hearers. Musical learning had done its utmost. Every kind of contrapuntal artifice had been brought into play. Without a pun, every score might be said to bristle with canon; canon in every interval, canon by augmentation and diminution, "per arsin et thesin," "per recte et retro." As to the words, there was not an attempt, any attempt indeed under such a system would have been idle, to bring out their meaning, to give them force, or to make them intelligible. In fact, the theorists had had their way; too much learning had made them mad, and the monstrous fabric they had raised collapsed from its own weight and want of proportion.

These evils, long and deeply felt, the subject of more than one papal bull, and doubtless of many an episcopal charge, at length came under the censure, first of the Council of Bâle, and subsequently of the Council of Trent, the execution of whose decrees so far as they concerned music, was delegated to a committee of eight persons, mostly singers in the Pope's chapel. The first proceeding of this committee was to forbid the performance, in future, of any Mass or Motet of which profane words formed an integral part; the second to banish equally from the service of the Church all music built on secular themes. These were, however necessary, sweeping measures; amounting practically, for the moment, to the undoing of the work of the last two hundred years. Virtually, all existing music was placed under an interdict. Worse than this, there was not only no music, but there were no models. A wonderful unanimity prevailed as to what Church music was not to be, but what it was to be was yet to seek. The cardinals appointed by the Pope to embody the Decrees of the Council of Trent (among them was no less a personage than San Carlo Borromeo) were desirous, above all things, that the text should be the principal consideration in all future settings of the sacred offices; and they suggested, as models, certain compositions of Constanzo Festa and of Palestrina, which however noble and however fit for their particular purpose, the more artistic portion of the committee knew to be too narrow in their scheme and too limited in their resources permanently to take the place of a style of music to which the faithful had long been used, and which, with all its faults, exhibited skill of a very remarkable kind, and was the work of men well trained in the art they pretended to practise.

The genius of Palestrina, though as yet immature, had attracted attention. To him was deputed the hard and at the moment all-important task of reconciling that which God had once joined, but which man had put asunder; of showing that the beautiful art he loved and practised had powers and resources yet unproved, and that it was not incompetent to the highest privilege of humanity—that of setting forth the glory of the Creator.

Palestrina applied to his task like one who knew himself to

be equal to a great occasion. He produced three Masses, the first two of which excited an amount of admiration altogether without precedent; the third settled the vexed question, as it would seem for all time, and at once saved music to the Church Catholic, and established a type which all the changes, enormous as they have been, that the musical art has known since his day (three centuries since) have failed to render less precious, less admirable, and even less admired. This is the work known as the "Missa Papæ Marcelli," the title of which has misled musical historians so long. It was so called as a tribute of gratitude, on the part of Palestrina, to the memory of one who had shown him kindness, but who had gone to his rest five* years before the occasion which called it into existence—*i.e.*, during the pontificate of Pius IV., in whose presence it was first performed, on the 19th of June, 1565.

Had Palestrina's career ended even at this moment, he would have left an impress on his age which no length of time or variety of circumstances could ever have effaced. The "Missa Papæ Marcelli" was not, however, a goal, but a starting-post. A long course lay before Palestrina. During the twenty-nine remaining years of his life he let no day pass without a line. The quantity is as astonishing as the quality of his productions. He did more, as well as better, than other men. The catalogue of his works is itself a work, and not a small one ; and it would be difficult to find any one of them without some point of interest, some passage carrying evidence of a master's hand. Would that it could be said that the world had repaid in any degree, during his lifetime, the debt that it owed, and acknowledged that it owed, to this great artist and, by all account, most estimable and most lovable man. His life was one long and

* A glance at a chronological table would have shown any one of the many writers who have passed on the ordinary and incorrect account of the composition and performance of this mass, that the events connected with it could not possibly have happened during the pontificate of Marcellus II., who, as we have seen, lived only *twenty* days after his election.

not very successful struggle for bare subsistence. He composed, directed, and taught unintermittingly; but his publications were unremunerative, his appointments meagre, and his scholars poor. No passage could be added to the "Calamities of Authors" more touching than the Epistle Dedicatory to one of his last publications, to Pope Sixtus V. It was of no avail. Palestrina had starved already through six pontificates; he was to starve through a seventh, and to die in harness, neglected and unresentful. His last words have been recorded. They were instructions to his son, the single one left to his old age, respecting the disposal of his unpublished works, which he solemnly charged him to give to the world with the least possible delay, "for the glory of the Almighty and His worship in the congregations of the faithful."

In the course of the second half of the sixteenth century the Italians not only learned from their Gallo-Belgian masters all they had to teach them, but turned their knowledge to new account, developing and invigorating old forms and inventing new ones. They became "wiser than their teachers," whose influence among them rapidly declined, and whose separate existence eventually ceased altogether.

To the genius and career of one more Gallo-Belgian musician, however, Roland de Lattre, better known by his Italianized name, Orlando di Lasso, I have still to call your attention, before finally taking leave of the great school of which he presents the most distinguished ornament. The date and even place of Roland de Lattre's birth have till very lately been matter of controversy. His most recent biographer, M. Delmotte,* would seem to have settled beyond doubt that he was born at Mons, in the year 1520, four years before Palestrina. Nothing has been recorded respecting his education, a fact the more to be regretted as, by the concurrent testimony of his

* "Notice Biographique sur Roland Delattre, connu sous le nom d'Orland de Lassus," par H. Delmotte. Valenciennes. 1835.

contemporaries, his general accomplishments were hardly exceeded by his musical. He is first presented to our notice as having, at the age of seventeen, attracted the attention of Ferdnando de Gonzaga, one of the soldiers of Charles V., who took him with him into Italy. At the end of a year Roland parted from Gonzaga, and accompanied Constanzio Castriotto to Naples, where he spent three years in the house of the Marquis de Terza, at the close of which he visited Rome, where he resided six months with the Archbishop of Florence, partly no doubt through whose influence he was appointed Maestro di Capella of St. John Lateran. He might easily have added another to the long list of illustrious Gallo-Belgians who lived and worked at this epoch in Rome; but the illness of his parents recalled him to Mons, which he reached too late to receive the last blessing of either. In company with a noble amateur, Cesare Brancaccio, he visited France and England, leaving nought but the bare record of the fact in either; after which we find him at Antwerp, where he remained two years. Whether he held any public office in this city is not stated, but his biographer tells us that he won the esteem and affection of all who approached him, not more by his musical talent and his general accomplishments, than by the simplicity of his character and the sweetness of his manners. His reputation spread far and wide. In 1557, Albert the Generous, Duke of Bavaria, invited him to his court, commissioning him at the same time to engage a number of native (Gallo-Belgian) musical performers, then deservedly esteemed the most skilful in Europe, for the service of the ducal chapel. At Munich De Lattre soon became as popular as a musician and as a man as he had been elsewhere. In 1558 he married Regina Weckinger, a lady of good family and attached to the court. Five years after this we find him at the head of the chapel, in the service of which no less than ninety-two musicians, vocal and instrumental, were at this time retained. Henceforth the reputation of De Lattre surpassed that of every contemporary save Palestrina, four years his junior. Sovereign princes strove with one another to do him honour. In 1570 the Emperor Maximilian granted to him and his descendants of both sexes "letters of nobility." Pope Gregory XIII. made him a Knight of the Order of St. Peter. The French King, Charles IX., made him a Knight of Malta, and on his visit to Paris in 1571, heaped favours of all kinds upon him; according to his host, Adrien Leroy, distinguished in his time no less as a musician than as a printer and publisher of music, solid ones among the number.* Struck by the beauty of De Lattre's music, more especially it is said by his setting of the Penitential Psalms, Charles IX. made strenuous efforts to win him to his service. His ducal patron strongly urged and eventually induced him, greatly against his own inclination, to accept the king's offers. He quitted Munich, but was met half way on his journey to Paris by the news of the king's death. He at once retraced his steps, was received by Albert with open arms, and reinstated in all his offices, with considerably increased emoluments. The decease (in 1579) of his munificent master and friend, however regretted, made no change in the outward circumstances of De Lattre. William V. (the Pious) proved as good a friend to him as his predecessor. He not only at once confirmed him in all his appointments, but subsequently presented him with an estate, and settled a pension on his wife, in the event of her outliving him. It is grievous to have to record that the sunshine of De Lattre's youth and manhood was not extended to his declining years. Whether from his continued and unintermittent labours as a composer, a director and a teacher, or from vexations arising out of some unsuccessful demands to be relieved of a portion of them, his powers, mental as well as bodily, suddenly gave way. After a partial

* In his dedication of a volume of Roland's compositions to the king, Leroy says, "Taceam munera plane regia quæ in Orlandum contulisti."

and happily brief aberration of intellect, he died in 1594—in the same year as Palestrina, the only one of his contemporaries who could, for invention, learning or renown, be for a moment compared with him.

Like two still more renowned, because more recent, contemporaries, Bach and Handel, of whom of course I shall have to speak later, De Lattre and Palestrina never met. It is impossible after reviews of both their careers, brief and imperfect as mine have necessarily been, not to compare and contrast them; that of the one so prosperous up to all but the very end, that of the other so adverse even till death. "Choyé, fêté partout," says Delmotte,* "De Lattre passait toutes ses journées avec les personnes les plus distinguées par leurs instruction, leur science, leur esprit et leur naissance." "La dedica," says Palestrina's biographer, of his volume of the Lamentations of Jeremiah to Sixtus V., "la dedica è un vero threno, una lamentazione, una flebile nenia delle somme miserie, cui andava soggetto il povero Giovanni."† Palestrina, it should be said, was unfortunate in his papal masters, many of whose predecessors and successors have been munificent patrons of genius and learning. The only one of them under whom he served, who showed practically any appreciation of his powers, Marcellus II., died as we have seen within a few days of his election. But "prosperity," says Lord Bacon, "is the blessing of the old dispensation, adversity of the new."

The general impression derived by those who have studied them from a comparison of the works of these two great musicians seems to be that in invention and fecundity, the latter always a characteristic of genius of the highest order, they are on a par; and that while Palestrina is the more learned, De Lattre is the more adventurous and therefore many-sided composer. In dignity, where the subject treated called for its

* "Notice Biographique," 24.

† "Vita di Pal." ii. 197.

manifestation, it would be impossible to decide between them. The one decided advantage of Palestrina over De Lattre is one which even the feeblest of his countrymen have always manifested over their northern contemporaries; sweetness of melody,—in an age of polyphonic music only to be manifested in the texture of individual parts.

Of the Italian contemporaries of Palestrina and De Lattre the most remarkable are the brothers Nanino and their pupil Anerio (Romans), Giovanni Gabrieli (a Venetian), and Luca Marenzio (a Lombard). The name of the latter is inseparably connected with a form of composition of which the origin is lost in obscurity, but which reached the highest perfection in his day and in his hands, the "Madrigal." The derivation of this word has been matter of controversy for two centuries and a half, and cannot even yet be considered as fixed. Some have traced it to the word Martegaux (*i.e.*, Provençaux), on the supposition that its form (of words rather than notes) is the invention of the poet-musicians of Provence. Others, seeking a pastoral origin for the thing itself, have derived it from *mandra*, a fold for cattle. I should be disposed rather to trace it to some form of hymn to the Blessed Virgin, possibly to the two words *Madre, gala*, or more likely still, *Alla Madre;* the letter *g* serving, on the inversion of the words, for euphony. This last hypothesis is supported by the fact that the Madrigal, though generally a secular composition, is not of necessity such; a large number of *Madrigali Spirituali* being extant the words of which, for the most part, have some reference to the Blessed Virgin.

Every composer of the latter part of the sixteenth century tried his hand on the Madrigal; the number of specimens which have come down to us is beyond all calculation. In the course of about forty years (from about 1570 to 1610) some hundreds, not of Madrigals, but of *Collections* of Madrigals issued from the press. In the fourteen years which connect 1587 and 1601 nine books or sets of them by Luca Marenzio alone were published in one city, Venice, not to speak of other places. Luca is said to have composed upwards of a thousand.

This activity, not merely of the pen but of the press, affords irrefragable evidence (were there none other) of the extent to which music was cultivated at this epoch. Music, like books, may be written from very various motives; it is most often printed from one only; expectation that it will sell. The printers (especially the Venetians) of the sixteenth century were, many of them, men of remarkable acquirements, and enthusiastic lovers of learning; but they were at the same time tradesmen, and in most cases very prosperous tradesmen, who would naturally and wisely prepare for sale what the mass of mankind wanted to buy.

There is reason to believe that this practical musical skill extended over every part of Europe having the slightest claim to be called civilized, during the latter part of the Second Period. Spain had, early in the sixteenth century, furnished the Italian choirs with excellent voices. Of Catholic Germany, as represented by Bavaria, I have already spoken. In Protestant Germany the influence of Luther, a musician and a lover of music, had been brought to bear on the cultivation of the art which he prized as "next to Divinity." Even Poland has to be added to the list of musical nations of this epoch; for the long sojourn of Luca Marenzio in that distant kingdom proves that it could then afford a home and find occupation for a great musician.

But on the Continent this widely spread executive skill was dependent for material on which to exercise itself almost entirely on Italian masters. From the middle of the sixteenth century the Gallo-Belgian school had declined in numbers and in influence year by year; the German school, since so pre-eminently great, can scarcely be said to have had any individual existence at that epoch; the beginnings of what we now understand by the French school were only made in the second half of the seventeenth century, and then, as we shall see, by a foreigner, an Italian. Of the Spanish school the rest of Europe knew then, and still knows, next to nothing.

The single exception to this dependence on "the foreigner," is presented by our own country. In the sixteenth century we not only sang and played as much and as well as our neighbours, but we sang and played our own music. It is no exaggeration to say that the English hold, and are recognised as holding, a very high place among the composers of the Second Period. Tallis, Farrant, Byrd, and Bevin, in "the service high and anthem clear;" Morley, Ward, Wilbye, and Weelkes in the madrigal; Bull, in performance as well as in composition; Dowland, "the friend of Shakspeare," in the part song; and, last and greatest in all styles, Orlando Gibbons:—these are all names to which the English musician may refer with confidence and with pride, as fit to be associated with those of Palestrina, De Lattre, and Marenzio. And moreover if the epithet "indigenous" could ever be rightly applied to any school of art, which is a question, the English school of music might put in a very strong claim to it. Our insular position, which has favoured us in so many things, has favoured us in the individuality of our music, and left our composers of earlier times more to their own resources than those of any other country. Indeed, a comparison of dates shows us to be rather the precursors than the followers of other nations. Among the theorists of the First Period, Bede (sixth and seventh centuries), John Cotton (eleventh century), and Hothby (fourteenth century) hold a very high place; and an Englishman, John Dunstable, so greatly influenced the art at the beginning of the fifteenth century, that the *invention of counterpoint* has been attributed to him,—absurdly, of course; but "where there is smoke, there is fire."

We have no composer of the fifteenth century to be put by

the side of Josquin Deprès and his Gallo-Belgian contemporaries; but in point of date we rather precede than follow the great Italians of the next century, *minus* the advantage of Gallo-Belgian teaching. In the year 1540, when Claude Goudimel set up the first music school in Rome, Christopher Tye was forty years of age, and Tallis twenty. The Italian and English Madrigal and Part-song writers synchronize as nearly as possible; Luca Marenzio and John Wilbye having been born probably in the very same year (1550) and Giovanni Gastoldi and John Dowland being exactly contemporary. A glance at the chronological tables at the end of this volume will show you other instances.

Whatever may have been the relative merits of the English and Italian composers of the Second Period, the duties of their several posterities have been far more reverently discharged towards the former than the latter. Periods have intervened during which the works of the English masters of the sixteenth century have experienced the neglect of their countrymen; but those periods have been brief, and the neglect has never been other than partial. No week, perhaps no day, passes over, without, in some one or more of our cathedral choirs, the voice of Tallis or of Gibbons being made to speak. But, save to a few enthusiasts, the music of Palestrina is as unfamiliar to his sensitive and gifted countrymen of the nineteenth century as is the music of Jubal. So with the Madrigalists. The works of Wilbye and many of his contemporaries are hardly less familiar to our generation than they were to their own; but the sweet notes of Marenzio—"Il più dolce cigno"—died out with the century in which they were first heard, and his compatriots have left their perpetuation to foreign voices and their record to foreign historians. Let us hope for better things with better days in Italy.

THE THIRD, OR TRANSITION, PERIOD.

FROM ABOUT A.D. 1600 TO ABOUT A.D. 1750.

THE SECOND PERIOD COMPARED WITH FOURTH—THEIR DIFFERENCES, OBVIOUS AND OCCULT—ANCIENT AND MODERN TONALITY—MODES, AUTHENTIC AND PLAGAL—ASSIMILATION OF ANCIENT AND MODERN TONALITY IN PRACTICE—*MI* CONTRA *FA*—ANCIENT AND MODERN HARMONY COMPARED—THE PERFECT CADENCE—ITS ANTIQUITY—THE NATURAL SCALE—THE RENAISSANCE, ITS EFFECTS ON MUSIC—DEFICIENCY OF EXPRESSION IN THE SCHOLASTIC MUSIC OF THE SECOND PERIOD—EARLY ATTEMPTS AT OPERA—THE FLORENTINE ACADEMY—BARDI, CORSI, STROZZI, AND GALILEO—PERI AND CACCINI—THE INNOVATIONS OF MONTEVERDE.

THE THIRD, OR TRANSITION, PERIOD

You will remember that I have divided the History of Music into Four Periods: that the First of these was a period rather of preparation for music than of music itself, in our sense of the word; that the Second was the period of the Old Masters; that the Fourth Period, in which we are living, is that of the Modern Masters; and that the Third, of which I have now to speak, was a Transitional Period connecting the Second and the Fourth.

This seems to be the time to explain in what essential particulars the music of the Old Masters, in its highest development, differs from that of our contemporaries. For in entering on this Third Period we step, as it were, on to a bridge connecting two opposite shores; and it is necessary that we should understand in what, besides mere position, the two districts it brings together are unlike, and what the difficulties of connecting them have been.

The differences between the music of the Second Period and that of the Fourth are of two kinds; the one obvious and easily explained, even to persons who know little about music; the other essentially technical and requiring for its appreciation a fair acquaintance with musical science, and for its thorough understanding a very close one.

Let us dispose of the first of these differences before we try to make anything of the second.

What I call the obvious differences between the music of

the Second Period and that of the Fourth, may be thus briefly described:—

Whereas the latter is of two kinds, vocal and instrumental, each of which has branched out into a very great variety of styles, the former, if not professedly, was actually of only one kind, vocal, and of only two or three styles, some so little unlike that it is hard to say in what they differ.

In modern times instrumental music has taken a place of its own, independent of, some would say above, vocal. Moreover, it has taken more forms than we have time to reckon. We have the symphony and the overture, for the full orchestra; the concerted piece for various numbers and sets of instruments; the duet, the trio, the quartet, &c. &c.; while the pianoforte, an instrument little more than a century old,* has given birth to a prodigious quantity of music of great variety as to form, character, length, and difficulty. And in vocal music, not only have we the purely vocal or unaccompanied form, in which the old masters are still in some respects our models, but we bring to the assistance of the voice any or all the resources of the modern orchestra, not to speak again of the pianoforte. It would be too much to say, that in the Second Period instrumental music had no existence; but, so far as we can judge of it, its status was altogether so inferior to that of vocal music, that, in a comparative estimate of the two periods, it may be safely left unregarded.

In the vocal compositions of the great masters of the Second Period we find no songs, or airs for a single voice; scarcely, indeed, anything analogous to the vocal solo of modern times. Nor do the vocal concerted pieces of the old masters present the variety of form and character to which we are now accustomed:

* Messrs. Broadwood and Sons, the eminent manufacturers of these instruments, have in their possession a play-bill, headed, "Covent Garden, May 16, 1767," which among other announcements contains the following, "Miss Brickler will sing a favourite song from Judith, accompanied by Mr. Dibdin on a *new* instrument call'd Piano Forte."

indeed, to an ear habituated exclusively to the sharp and striking contrasts of contemporary music, their works appear at first wonderfully like one another. So they are; but they are wonderfully different from one another also. The fault is in us, not in them:—

> "Facies non omnibus una
> Nec diversa tamen, qualem decet esse sororum."

Palates habituated to ardent spirits and Cayenne pepper are not generally very apt in discriminating delicate wines or simple viands; and we shall have little chance of understanding or feeling, still less of liking, the music of the Second Period, unless we try it by standards very different from those we apply to the music of our own time. I have no desire that a general revival of the style of this period should be attempted. The result of such an attempt would certainly be a quantity of very stiff, very unreal, and very unoriginal music. But composition is one thing, performance another. We have discovered (not very long since) that there were painters before the age of Leo X.; and we now willingly find places for their works in our public collections, and for duplications of them on our own walls. Does any one in his senses admire Raphael or Rubens the less, because he has made acquaintance with Fra Angelico and Van Eyk? The modern musician is like a man with an ancestry of four centuries, who ignores even his grandfather. Far be it from me to claim places in our musical Pantheon for Palestrina and Marenzio *above* those of Mozart and Beethoven; but I do claim places for these Patriarchs of Harmony *beside* those of their descendants. I do not pretend that the old music is better than the new. What I am anxious to impress upon you is that it is essentially different from it, another form of art; and that in neglecting to perform it, and in refusing to listen to it, the modern musical student maintains a condition of mind that not only shuts him out from a large circle of enjoyment, but actually prevents his estimating as he ought to do even the music to which he limits his sympathy and attention, that of his own time.

But we must pass on to the consideration of the more occult, because more technical, differences between ancient and modern music.

Every musical passage is referable to, or must form part of, some succession of sounds which have a certain appreciable relation to one another; one of these sounds being the fixed point or basis on which these relations ultimately depend. Such a succession of sounds has been called by the various names of tone, mode, scale, and key; the first of these names giving to the fixed point the name tonic, and the last, that of key-note. In strictness of speech, a scale and a mode are not at all the same thing, though they are inseparable things; and we shall consult clearness by distinguishing them. A scale is a succession of steps leading from a given sound to its octave. But those steps are of unequal sizes; and on the places of the smaller ones depends the mode. In modern music we have but two modes, the major and the minor; that kind of scale wherein the semitones fall between the 3rd and 4th sounds, and that wherein they fall between the 2nd and 3rd. Or, to put the case in another way, there are only two sounds in our "natural" scale which we can recognise as tonics or key-notes, the first sound C, and the sixth A; the scale constructed on the latter of these requiring occasional modification in two places, to satisfy the modern ear.

Fig. 16.

Now the old masters had theoretically no less than seven, and indeed, as we shall see, fourteen modes. For their theory would have permitted the use of every note of the natural scale as a tonic, and the building upon it of a succession of sounds limited to that scale. They did not alter sounds by sharps or flats, as we do, to make scales beginning on whatever sound like one another (*i.e.*, to make the semitones fall in the same places); but they left the sounds of the "natural" scale as they found them, and thus produced a set of seven scales, no two of which are alike, because in no two do the semitones fall in the same places. See Fig. 17, wherein the seven primitive modes occupy the *left* side.

Connected with each of these scales, which were called "authentic," was another, its "plagal" (see the *right* side of Fig. 17), which raised the whole possible number to fourteen. An intimate relation exists between each authentic mode and its plagal; for the 5th sound of every authentic scale is the 1st of its plagal, while (*vice versâ*) the 4th of every plagal scale is the 1st of its authentic; this last note being the "final," or as we should now say, the "tonic" of both.

THE FOURTEEN (Possible) MODES.

Fig. 17.

AUTHENTIC. PLAGAL.

Melodies in authentic modes were considered more dignified in character than those in plagal. This, I think, might be admitted in respect to modern melodies accidentally conformable to ancient rule. There is a certain stateliness about a melody that lies between a key-note and its octave, rarely found in one lying between the 5th of the key and its octave. Listen to these two melodies, the first plagal, the second authentic. I think you will award the palm of sweetness to the one, of strength to the other.

EVENING HYMN. (PLAGAL.)

Fig. 18.

CHORALE—"EIN' FESTE BURG."* (AUTHENTIC.)

Fig. 19.

* There are three different arrangements of this noble melody in the "Vierstimmige Choralgesänge," von J. S. Bach. Leipsig, bei Breitkoff und Härtel, pp. 16, 145, 158.

Some of the (possible) modes in Fig. 17 were never, and others little, used. Thus the scale beginning on B was unavailable, from its imperfect fifth; and that beginning on F, from its pluperfect fourth or tritone. Nor did the old tonality recognise the scale beginning on C, our "natural" scale. By flattening the fourth sound, B, of the scale beginning on F, the old masters produced a true diatonic major scale, as we should call it; but the scale of C, our model scale, formed no part of their system. Even the scale beginning on A, our model minor scale, was not recognised by them.*

Practically then the number of scales available under the old systems was but eight, four authentic, four plagal; one of the former, the scale of F (V. of Fig. 17) being admissible only by the alteration of B, its 4th sound, to B flat. Even of these eight some were much more used than others. With the English composers of the Second Period the first tone, that of which D is the final, seems to have been the favourite. The Service by Tallis, and the Anthem, "Call to Remembrance," by Farrant, with others in the well-known collection of Dr. Boyce, are fine and thoroughly characteristic examples of this mode. A composition in the seventh tone, the Canon "Non nobis Domine," attributed to Byrd (d. 1623) is still popular.

In this variety of modes the old masters may seem to have had greatly the advantage over the modern who, by the reduction of the number from eight to two, have had their resources apparently much diminished. That such is the case has been and is maintained by some writers who, regardless of the instincts of humanity, believe that the practice of the Second Period was perfectly consistent with its theory, and that the *written* music of the fifteenth and sixteenth centuries represents literally that which any set of people could ever have been made to sing, or any other set of people induced to listen to. I believe the musical practices of our forefathers to have been

* The tonics of VI. and II. (Fig. 17) are not C and A, but F and D.

very inconsistent with, and very superior to, their musical theories; and that an unintermittent feud was maintained between the theoretical and practical musicians of the Second Period, and that it is to the victory of the latter that we owe modern tonality.

Modern musicians, as you all know, spare no pains to prevent misunderstanding, and thereby misrepresentation, of their productions, in performance. In a piece of music, now-a-days, the duration and pitch of every sound are presented beyond the possibility of mistake, by means of our now perfected musical notation. Nay, more; an extensive vocabulary or, more properly, hotch-potch, of words gathered from almost every European language, is at the disposal of the composer, who is thus enabled to indicate the style in which he desires a movement, or any individual portion of it, to be performed. We have, *Vivace, Slow, Da Capo, Bis, With Expression, Legato, Détaché,* and even *Langsam* and *Sehr Frisch.* There is an instrument (the metronome) by the use of which the composer may indicate the pace of every movement to the greatest nicety. Now, a good deal of this apparatus has come into general use only in this century, and none of it had existence till the beginning of the Third Period. Not only were "marks of expression"* quite unknown when the old musical systems prevailed, but many contrivances were then non-existent, or not yet adopted, without which it is difficult to conceive musical performance going on at all. For instance, up to the beginning of the seventeenth century, music was universally printed without bars; those, to us, indispensable helps. But this is nothing. Hundreds of volumes of music of the Second Period exist, without a sharp or flat in them (accidental or other) from beginning to end. The first impression derived from this fact is that the theory of the ancient modes forbidding anything

* Roland De Lattre is said by some historians to have used them. I have not been able to confirm this statement.

like our free use of the chromatic scale, passages which we could only perform by doing intolerable violence to our musical instincts were executed as a matter of course by singers trained in another school, and habituated to another musical idiom. Tradition however comes to the support of common sense in this matter, and shows that the instincts of the singers of the sixteenth century were very much akin to those of the singers of the nineteenth. A number of rules for the alteration of notes (by sharp or flat) during performance have come down to us the observance of which must practically have approximated the old tonality to ours much more nearly than the written music would lead us to believe possible.

These rules are nearly all to be traced to that abhorrence of the interval of the tritone which found expression in the old apothegm "*Mi* (B) *contra Fa* (F) *diabolus est.*" A passage like Fig. 20 could never have been sung as it is written; the B (second bar) in the soprano is "in false relation with" (*i.e.*, a tritone above) the F of the alto; and the B in the bass in false relation with the F in the tenor. Moreover, a phrase was rarely allowed to end on a minor chord. The third sound (from the bass) might be omitted altogether, but if inserted, it was generally major.*

Fig. 20.

Every B, therefore, in Fig. 20, would be made flat, and the C in the last chord sharp; as in Fig. 21.

* This practice was generally observed up to the middle of the last century. I. S. Bach almost invariably closes his movements with a major chord.

Fig. 21.

But granting that the instincts of the singers of the Second Period suggested many effects which the principles of the composers forbade *their* recognising, by introducing them into their scores, it is quite certain that those principles gave rise to a style of harmony essentially different from ours, and from which no conceivable modifications made during performance could eradicate the possibly harsh but indisputably stately character. I use the word "harmony" as representing the successive results of an accumulation of parts. For of a chord, as an isolated fact, the old masters took little account. They were not harmonists at all, in our sense of the word, but contrapuntists; laying melody upon melody, according to certain laws, but uncognizant of, or indifferent to, the effects of their combinations as they successively came upon the ear. Their construction was horizontal, not perpendicular. They built in layers, and their music differs from most of ours as a brick wall does from a colonnade. To return to this "harmony." If there be any one principle which more strongly governs a modern musician than another it is this; that those combinations follow one another with the best effect which are, or might be, connected together by common notes. Thus, the progression from the chord of C to that of F is an acceptable and a common one; because C, which is the 8ve of the first chord, is also the 5th to the second. (Fig. 22.) While a progression like that from the chord of C to that of D is an exceptional one (with us), because the two chords have *no* common note. (Fig. 23.)

Fig. 22.

Fig. 23.

Ancient and modern harmony are however best contrasted when used subserviently to the same idea; in the treatment, for example, of a given melody, or passage of melody.

Look at Fig. 24; it is a fragment of melody of unknown antiquity.

STABAT MATER.

Fig. 24.

Every modern musician would not, of course, treat this or any other passage in exactly the same manner; but Fig. 25 may pass as an average arrangement of it, in as modern a style as its nature will allow.

STABAT MATER.

Fig. 25.

Now look at,* and listen to, Palestrina (Fig. 26).

Fig. 26. G. P. DE PALESTRINA.

* I did not know on first presenting this contrast that I had been anticipated in it by Oulibicheff, whose "Nouvelle Biographie de Mozart" (v. *infra*) was then unknown to me.

Could a page of *Isaiah* and a smart newspaper article be more unlike? I do not ask which of these two harmonizations you like the better, but whether two such astonishingly different results must not have been wrought out of the same material, by processes of thought and modes of operation wide as the poles asunder. One cause of difference in our practice I have already pointed out,—that the old masters looked to the relation of super-imposed parts rather than to the relations of successive combinations. But a more direct cause must be sought in their view of a scale or key. This was inevitably indistinct; as is shown by the absence from their works of a figure or effect so familiar to us, and so simple in itself, that it is difficult to conceive a time in which, or a set of musicians to whom, it was not familiar. I speak of the figure known as the perfect cadence or close, produced by the resolution of the discord of the dominant seventh on the chord of the tonic.

Fig. 27.

In these two chords are included every note but one of the scale to which they belong—C, D, E, F, G, and B. More than this; the first combination can only exist in one scale, that of C. The F natural proves that that scale has no sharps; the B natural that it has no flats. The combination of these two notes, F and B, is not merely the characteristic, but the spring and source, of modern harmony. From the moment that its power was felt, music became, if not altogether a new language, certainly a new idiom; and an idiom so much richer, so much more nervous, so much more flexible than its predecessor, that the desuetude of the latter became only a question of time.

The discovery of the perfect cadence can hardly be attributed to any individual. It was doubtless heard in popular music ages before its existence was recognised by the learned. That such was the case with our "natural" scale (not, as we have seen, one of the received ancient modes) we know from inspection of such specimens of secular melody as we considered at our last meeting. Moreover, some of the earliest of the Belgian masters seem to have been more often drawn towards it than their immediate successors. Thus the *Stabat Mater* of Josquin Deprès (who died at least ten years before Palestrina was born) is unequivocally in the key of F, each part ending with a perfect cadence·

Fig. 28 is the ending of the first division, and Fig. 27 that of the second, of this fine composition. The chord of the dominant in Fig. 28 is accompanied, though timidly, by the seventh,—the F in the alto part, resolved on the E in the last bar. So in Fig. 29 (bar 2) the B flat in the soprano is the seventh to C, and resolved (in the last bar) on A.

PERFECT CADENCES FROM JOSQUIN DEPRÈS.

Fig. 28.

Fig. 29.

My attention was drawn to these cadences by a very apposite and interesting passage in the "Institutione Harmoniche" of Zarlino, a great theorist of the sixteenth century. He says of our key of C (which he calls the first mode), "It is spoken of as well adapted for dances; since the greater number of those we hear now in Italy are set in this mode; whence it has arisen that in our days some call it '*il modo lascivo.*' And," he continues, "many *cantaline* in the same mode are found in ecclesiastical books, chiefly in the more ancient." And again, "modern composers (he speaks of Palestrina and his own contemporaries) have even set in this mode an almost infinite variety of every kind of cantaline, such as masses, hymns, &c., and other kinds of *canzoni*, among which are found the *Stabat Mater* of Giosquino, and an infinite number of others to which it would be useless to refer."

That Josquin was at all aware of the importance of the natural scale, or of the powers of the perfect cadence, it is impossible to believe. His training and the circumstances in which he was placed were too strong for his instincts, which, had he been able to give them fair play, might have altered the whole history of music. An entire century, however, was still to elapse before the contemned *modo lascivo* and its complement the perfect cadence were to obtain their rights—a hearing. It is consistent with all experience that they should have done so through the instrumentality of one of those irregularly educated men of genius without whose co-operation no great changes in the world are brought about.

The earliest confessed innovator on, the first declared rebel against, the old constitutions was Claudio Monteverde, born between 1565 and 1570, at Cremona, eminent even at that time for the excellence of its stringed instruments. To give an account of his innovations and explain their successful issue, we must not merely retrace our steps a little, but, as it may seem, quit the road which lay open before us.

In the last years of the fifteenth century a variety of causes combined to direct attention in Western Europe to the language and literature of Greece and, as a necessary consequence, to what is called by grammarians the "harmony" of language. I need not tell you that this was but one of many subjects the consideration of which were both causes and effects of the prodigious movement known as *The Renaissance;* a movement which eventually brought about changes in the condition of the world only inferior in extent and importance to those consequent on the promulgation of Christianity itself. Nor is it my business now to direct more than a passing thought towards the effects of this movement on architecture, sculpture and painting. The least acquainted with the history of these arts knows something of the good and the evil represented by this word Renaissance; of the mighty works to which it gave birth, and of the mighty works to which it dealt death, and worse than death, obloquy, only now beginning to fall back on itself.

But the effect of this prodigious action of moral and intellectual forces on Music is a part, and one of the most curious and interesting parts, of the subject before us. The Renaissance left an impress of music, but that impress was not its own impress; it did something to it, but not what it intended. The reason is plain. The poetry, architecture, sculpture, and painting of the later Middle Ages were not new arts. They were, it is true, the expression of an unprecedented condition of the world; but, as outward and visible signs, they were simply varieties of what had been done ages before, and done magnificently. The "Divine Comedy" was liable at any moment to comparison with the "Iliad," the cathedral of Chartres with the Parthenon, the works of the mediæval sculptors with those of the age of Pericles.

But the music of modern Europe is a new art. There is not the slightest evidence to show that anything analogous to it existed among the nations of antiquity. So far from the more polished of these having practised what we call "harmony," it remains even to be proved that the vocal melody of the Greeks consisted of anything more strictly musical than "intoning." It is improbable that the music of the Hebrews was essentially different from, or at all superior to, that of the Greeks. The so-called music of modern Asiatics is, for the most part, simply intolerable to a European ear.

Now this the scholars and artists of the Renaissance could not know, could not perhaps have been made to believe. It was altogether consistent with opinion and practice in the fifteenth and sixteenth centuries to look back to the best time of Greek art for principles and examples in music, as well as in poetry, architecture, sculpture, and painting. The results, however, of this retrospection were altogether disproportionate to the pains it involved. That which had never been born could not be born again. A renaissance of Greek music was impossible; simply because no such thing, in our sense of the word, had ever existed. Scholars and *savants* might succeed in teaching their deluded disciples to look on the sculptures of Rheims or the frescoes of Pisa as products of an age of barbarism; but they could not make them insensible to the majesty of Palestrina or the sweetness of Luca Marenzio. Moreover, this new art had called into existence a new science, and a new class of scholars and *savants* who, if they were incompetent to appeal to the intellects of their hearers, could appeal to their hearts in "notes of linked sweetness long drawn out"—"sounds and sweet airs that give delight and hurt not."

The action of the Renaissance on music was altogether unlike that on the other arts. It failed in exciting a revolution, but it induced the commencement of a bit-by-bit reform, which, consummated only in the middle of the last century, occupied what I have called the Third, or "Transition" Period.

The Church, as we have seen, had something to complain of in the music of the Second Period. So had the world.

Noble and even elegant as this music often was, it by no means fulfilled the conditions of a perfect art. It would seem to have exhausted all its resources and was still open to grave and well-grounded objection. It was wanting in that quality or power which the learned and unlearned, in all arts alike, prize more highly than any other—expression.

This deficiency, eventually due to the cause I have already dealt with, an uncertain tonality, is immediately due to an equally uncertain rhythm, the result of a timid application, or absolute neglect, of the laws of quantity and accent, in the adjustment of words to music. That "vagueness" which strikes the modern ear in listening to the old music, and to which it is impossible to deny a certain charm, is not, as has been fondly supposed, the result of any æsthetical principle, but simply of incapability in the old masters to strike the ear in any other way. There is no deficiency of rhythm in the popular tunes of this, and much earlier, epochs. The "modo lascivo" is the "scale of nature," and time is, perhaps, older than tune. The makers of popular tunes, the jongleurs, the minstrels, the people themselves, threw them off with utter unconcern about the laws of the schools; and the disciples of the schools, unhappily, refused to turn the happy inspirations of these unlearned folk to account.

The practical spirit of the Renaissance had hit this blot in the music of the Second Period early in the sixteenth century. While the great Italian composers had been developing the resources of their own art in compositions differing in no essential principle from those of their Belgian predecessors, the scholars and students of antiquity had been scraping together the fragments, few and undecypherable, of Greek music; quite unconscious of or indifferent to the fact, that in the music of their own epoch lay the material for an art which was afterwards to achieve all that they desired, and a great deal more than they could ever have conceived desirable.

The first attempts at this Musical Renaissance were made, as might have been expected, in connexion with dramatic representation, which, even in our era, is of very ancient date; the earliest dramas being on subjects connected with Holy Writ. These were always interspersed with, or accompanied by, music of some kind or other.*

The oldest secular dramatic piece which has yet been discovered, of which music is an integral part, is the comic opera of Adam de la Hale, "Li Gieus de Robin et de Marion," of which I gave some account at our last meeting. This was, perhaps, not a solitary production of the best age of Gothic art; but, I believe, none of equal importance has yet been brought to light.

We must pass on to the first years of the Renaissance for another specimen, the libretto of which is from the pen of the eminent poet and scholar Politian, the tutor of Pope Leo X. This "hasty production of two days" was called "Orfeo," another of those subjects on which artists seem never weary of trying their skill. It was performed for the entertainment of Cardinal Gonzaga of Mantua, at Florence, in 1475.

Other essays were made in the course of the next century, of none of which we have more than a bare record. Thus a Pastoral Drama called "Il Sacrifizio" was set to music by Alfonso della Viola, and performed at the Court of Henry II. of France, in 1555. And in 1574 an opera, the composition of the great theorist Zarlino, is said to have been performed at Venice when Henry III. passed through that city on his way from Poland to France, after the death of Charles IX. These and other contemporary works must inevitably have been composed in the madrigalesque style, with little or no attempt at dramatic colouring or expression of the sense of the words. It was not till the very end of the sixteenth century that any such

* See M. de Coussemaker's "Drames Liturgiques du Moyen Age," Paris, 1861.

attempt was made to realize these to us indispensable conditions of the musical drama.

About the year 1580 a number of amateurs living in Florence, dissatisfied with the relations heretofore existing between poetry and music, formed themselves into a Society or Academy for promoting the closer union of the two arts, by the revival of the "musical declamation of the Greeks." Their posterity, our ancestors, have gratefully and justly handed some of their names down to us. The most distinguished of them were Giovanni Bardi, Giacomo Corsi, and Berardo Strozzi, an eminent Dominican preacher. With these were associated Vincenzio Galileo (father of the great Galileo Galilei), who, at one of their meetings, produced and performed a setting of his own of the episode "Ugolino," from the "Divine Comedy." This first attempt at monody has, I believe, not been preserved; but it would appear to have made a great sensation at the time of its production, and to have confirmed those who heard it in the hypothesis they had set up in respect to music "after the manner of the ancients." A few years later, Emilio del Cavaliere, a Roman gentleman, produced, in the presence of the Grand Duke of Tuscany, Ferdinand de' Medici, two dramas with music, "Il Satiro," and "La Disperazione di Fileno." Other works of the same kind followed, or accompanied, these. The poet Rinuccini wrote, and the musician Peri set, a pastoral called "Dafne;" and a lyric tragedy, "Il Morte di Euridice," in the setting of which Peri was aided by a contemporary musician, Caccini, was performed at Florence (in 1600), on the occasion of the marriage of Henry IV. of France with Maria de' Medici. The names of those who took part in this performance have been preserved. They appear to have been, one and all, instrumentalists as well as vocalists, amateurs and persons of rank.

These attempts, however, were soon surpassed in the works of a new candidate for distinction in this style of music, Claudio

Monteverde. The first compositions of this musician were in no way distinguished from those of his contemporaries, save in their somewhat clumsy or slovenly texture. Like Palestrina and Luca Marenzio, he tried his "'prentice hand" on motets and madrigals; unlike those great masters, with but little success. Distinction in that walk of art might or might not have been any longer accessible, at the end of the sixteenth century; but Monteverde's failure would hardly have settled the question. The event however proved that, though unable from his deficient scholarship to perpetuate an old thing, he had musical invention and force of character to institute a new one. Had Monteverde been a more regularly educated musician, he would probably have added one more to the long list of forgotten writers of irreproachable music which nobody cares to hear. As it was, his very deficiencies, of which so intelligent a person must have been thoroughly aware, might have suggested to him the possibility of making a career where they would be much less sensibly felt. Whatever his purely musical resources may have been, in comparison with the great contrapuntists of the end of the sixteenth century, they must have been enormous as compared with those of his associates, the ingenious but superficial searchers after the music of the Greeks,—about which music there was perhaps little to be ascertained, and about which certainly nobody succeeded in ascertaining anything. An amateur among artists, Monteverde must have found himself an artist among amateurs; and the results of his experiments in Greek music, however little Greek, were at once acknowledged as more successful than any yet made with the same end. His melody proved more symmetrical, his rhythm more strongly marked, his harmony more pure, and his instrumentation fuller and more varied. A much less lively imagination would easily have enabled him to turn these resources to account in the production of dramatic effects unknown before his time. I have never seen an original copy of any one of Monteverde's operas, so that I am not in a condition to report upon them as entire works. Extracts from them are, however, to be found in several histories and collections. For instance, Sir John Hawkins gives an account,* confirmed by other authorities, of the most important of Monteverde's dramatic productions, a "favola in musica" called *Orfeo.* In the performance of this work as many as thirteen different instruments were used; and as some of these were multiplied by two, three, four, and in one instance ten, the orchestra amounted to the respectable number of thirty-six. Unlike modern operatic composers, who generally get the utmost possible amount of noise out of their orchestras before their audiences are fairly seated, Monteverde never uses his instruments *en masse*, but only in groups of two or three, and on no occasion of more than ten. The number and quality of the instruments distinguish the person or persons whom they accompany. Thus *Orfeo* is always supported by "duoi contrabassi da viola;" *Euridice* by "duoi chitaroni;" *Pluto* by "quattro tromboni;" and *Speranza* by "duoi piccoli violini alla francese." There is an overture, or toccata, to this opera "for a trumpet and other instruments" of which, whatever might be its merits, sustaining power was not one. It consists of eight bars, which (so it is directed) are to be played through three times before the rising of the curtain. The specimen of recitative, or "declamation after the manner of the ancients," quoted by Sir John Hawkins, might have had some interest given to it by a mode of performance the tradition of which is now lost; but, as it stands on paper, it is insufferably tiresome. It consists of a dialogue between Apollo and Orpheus who, besides extending their observations to a length insupportable, it might have seemed, to human patience, exhibit, in the music which is the vehicle of them, a contempt for the laws of musical grammar which, however consistent with their rank as heathen

* "History of Music," vol. iii. p. 430.

deities, is productive of results simply unendurable to human ears. Nothing can show more clearly how thoroughly the Academy at the Palazzo Vernio had possessed Monteverde with one idea than the utter absence, not merely of musical rhythm, but of musical form of any kind, in these specimens. That which is called "air" is hardly distinguishable from that which is called "musica parlante" or recitative. Yet at this time the streets of Florence, the canals of Venice, and the vineyards of Orvieto must have been ringing with clear, simple, sharply cut tune, and every church in Italy must have echoed daily with models of declamatory music of which the average execution would probably have been, though not then at its very best, still excellent. But history abounds with proofs of the difficulty of bit-by-bit improvement, especially from within. But for the efforts of the Florentine Academy, the progress of the musical art, which perhaps had gone as far as it could in one direction, might have been checked for centuries. Corsi and his friends have been well compared by more than one modern historian to the alchemists and the astrologers of the Middle Ages. They found neither the philosopher's stone, nor the connexion between human events and the courses of the stars, but they did much for the real sciences of chemistry and astronomy. So with the Florentine Academy. They proposed to call into existence a new art. They failed in this inevitably. But they called the attention of those who prized, because they understood, music as then practised, to its deficiencies, and set them in the right way to remove them. Wonderful is it, but not less true, that in the efforts of a few superficial *dilettanti*, incited rather by the love of literature than of music, we have the origin of a movement which has given us the magnificent unmixed music of the modern symphonic school. Equally wonderful and equally true is it that without this movement, in its origin, intention, and forms of expression, essentially pagan, the world might still have wanted the grandest of all productions of Christian art—the modern Oratorio.

THE THIRD, OR TRANSITION, PERIOD

(*Continued*).

CLAUDIO MONTEVERDE—HIS "NEW EFFECTS"—CARISSIMI—HIS RECITATIVE—INSTRUMENTAL PERFORMANCE—MUSICAL INSTRUMENTS, "BOWED" AND "WIND"—TEMPERAMENT—THE ORGAN—OTHER KEYED INSTRUMENTS—INSTRUMENTAL MUSIC—CORELLI—THE SCARLATTI FAMILY—ALESSANDRO SCARLATTI—THE FRENCH SCHOOL—THE "ACADÉMIE"—LULLY—MUSIC IN ENGLAND—THE RESTORATION—THE "CHILDREN" OF THE CHAPEL ROYAL—PELHAM HUMPHREY — PURCELL — HANDEL — HIS OPERAS AND ORATORIOS—HIS PLAGIARISMS—JOHN SEBASTIAN BACH—HIS "WOHL-TEMPORIRTE CLAVIER."

THE THIRD, OR TRANSITION, PERIOD

(Continued).

FEW things are more difficult to verify than the claims of inventors. The more closely we look into the history of art or science the more hesitation we feel in ascribing to this or that individual this or that discovery. Certain it is that every great name covers some other name that ought to be great; and that almost every discovery has been hinted at (if not more) by some predecessor, or even contemporary, of him who has been so fortunate as to associate himself with it in the public mind. I have found so many instances of this in my own department of history, that I feel sometimes very doubtful as to the fact of anybody having really invented anything. Our work would be easier were it otherwise. For example, a great deal of trouble would be saved us could we honestly assign to Claudio Monteverde all the inventions which the makers and retailers of musical memoirs attribute to him.

It must be admitted however that, though Monteverde did not invent the perfect cadence, he was the first to appreciate its importance, and to turn it to account in others beside the natural scale. Several combinations and progressions proposed by him have, it is true, neither been justified by modern theory nor incorporated into modern practice. (See Figs. 30 and 31, *a*, *b*, *c*, *d*.) Others, on the contrary, which he would seem to have used for the first time have found universal acceptance. (See Fig. 31, *e*, *f*.)

EXAMPLES OF MONTEVERDE'S NEW EFFECTS.

From the Madrigal* "Straccia mi pur il Core."

Fig. 30.

From the Madrigal† "Cruda Amarilli."

Fig. 31.

* Copies of these madrigals are to be found in Martini's "Saggio Fondamentale Pratico di Contrappunto." Bologna, 1774.

† Ibid.

It would be ungracious therefore, testing him however severely, to deny Monteverde's right to be regarded as one of the greatest benefactors of the musical art, or to consider his epoch as anything short of the turning-point of the history of modern music. Certainly during the career of no other musician that can be named, of like reputation and influence, were such great and important changes in musical practice made. His life was prolonged beyond average duration; he had attained the age of at least eighty years when (in 1649) it was brought to a close. But, as we sometimes find with men of this class, the particular work which he seems to have been sent into the world to do was begun late and finished early. His Third Book of Madrigals, in which are found some of his first innovations, was not published till 1598, when he must have been at least thirty-five years of age, and he does not appear to have made any important addition to his inventions after the year 1624, when he was but sixty-three. So that his career may be brought into the small compass of a quarter of a century. Monteverde never carried out his own ideas to their ultimate consequences. Perhaps it was impossible, within the compass of one life, to do so; more probably he was incompetent to the task under any circumstance. His career therefore was that of a conqueror, not of a colonist; of a pioneer, not of a settler. The territory of which he had for a moment taken possession was to be brought under cultivation by others; among these by an artist born some twenty years later than Monteverde, and destined to survive him by a still larger number. This longest-lived of the long-lived fraternity of musicians rejoiced in the tender and well-sounding name of *Carissimi;* and one of the few facts known about him is that he well deserved it. It is much to be regretted that we have so little information about the training and subsequent career of so great a musician and so good a man; especially as there is reason to believe that a good deal more might be obtained from certain memoirs relating to the masters of the Roman school which are still in MS. in the Vatican Library.

Giacomo Carissimi was born at Padua about the year 1582, and he is believed to have learnt the rudiments of music in that strong and erudite city. His works contain evidence that neither was his science obtained nor his taste formed in the Roman school, but rather in that of Venice, where Zarlino in the theory and Gabrieli in the practice of musical composition, had long been pursuing a course as independent of that of the rest of Italy as was the policy of the republic under which they lived. But who, among the many excellent musicians then living in Venice and the neighbouring towns, had the honour of being the instructor of Carissimi has not yet been ascertained. We are equally uninformed how or where he passed his early manhood. Kircher, who printed his "Musurgia" at Rome in the year 1649, tells us that he had then been for many years the esteemed musical director (*præfectus dignissimus*) of the church of St. Apollinaris, connected with the German college; and Mattheson, an eminent German musical critic who wrote in the early part of the next (the eighteenth) century, ascertained that Carissimi was still living in Rome in the year 1672, when he must have been at least eighty-five. The precise year of his death is unknown.

Carissimi, it is believed, never wrote for the theatre, and

comparatively seldom even for the Church. A few Masses are the only known specimens of his Service Music. He is the earliest great master of the Sacred Cantata in its many and various forms. He was the first musician, competent to turn the discovery to account, who perceived the scope afforded for the new musical resources opened up by Monteverde and his associates, in the form of composition attempted in the preceding century by Animuccia at the suggestion of St. Filippo Neri, the Oratorio. Among the many examples of this, the noblest form which modern art has taken, left by Carissimi, is his "Jephtha," of which I gave a public performance, some years since, at St. Martin's Hall. The choruses in this Oratorio have been surpassed not unfrequently by composers who have been so fortunate as to have had Carissimi for their point of departure; but few even among these have surpassed his recitative, nor indeed often equalled it. This kind of composition must have had a particular fascination for Carissimi. For movements requiring development he lived at an unfortunate epoch. The music of the old masters had lost its hold on the public ear; and the time was not yet come for exhibiting their sustained grandeur in anything so different from it in detail as the music of the Transition Period inevitably was. But there was nothing to prevent recitative, in the hands of any musician of genius who had a feeling for language, reaching something very like perfection, at once. Such a musician was Carissimi; and his recitative is, in point of musical construction, accent, and fitness for the voice, as near perfection as may be.

These lectures have an object with which practical illustrations would in many ways seriously interfere. But I cannot refrain from singing you (you are not likely to hear it on any other occasion) a fragment of Carissimi's recitative, now at least two centuries old, and about a century older than any similar music of Handel, with whose compositions of this class we are all of us familiar.

It is singular that this Oratorio, which is not only interesting historically and full of beautifully elaborated thoughts, but very short, should never have been printed. Extracts from it are to be found in Rochlitz's *Sammlung vorsüglicher Gesangstücke;** but the only complete copy to which I can refer you is among the musical MSS. left by Dean Aldrich to the Library of Christ Church, Oxford.†

The passage I have selected forms part of the scene in which Jephtha is met by his daughter on his return from victory. The words (slightly altered from the "Vulgate")‡ will tell the rest.

RECITATIVE, BY CARISSIMI.

FROM THE ORATORIO, "JEPHTHA."

Fig. 32.

* Schott, Mainz.

† A volume containing four oratorios by Carissimi, "Jephtha," "The Judgment of Solomon," "Jonah," and "Belshazzar," has, since this was written, been edited by Chrysander.

‡ Judic. xi.

Before I speak of one service said to have been rendered to music by Carissimi, I must direct your attention to a department of musical practice which began to assume individual importance only towards the end of the seventeenth century, but which had become a valuable adjunct much earlier, and which was both a cause and an effect of many of the changes music underwent during the Second Period. I mean instrumental performance.

We have seen that even at the close of the sixteenth century an orchestra of no less than thirty-six performers was employed in Monteverde's "Orfeo;" but that these were only used two or three at a time, never *en masse*. This was not altogether a matter of choice, for the nature of many of the instruments forbad their being used in concert. It is obvious that there must exist a certain balance in the intensity, and a certain suitableness or sympathy in the quality, of different instruments, before they can be used together effectively. To put an extreme case, you can hardly conceive a quartet for a violin, a flute, a viola, and a trombone. Nor would a mandolin, or even a guitar, have much chance of obtaining a hearing accompanied by an ordinary regimental band. Indeed, instruments far less discrepant than these can only be efficiently combined under particular conditions of musical composition. It has now been ascertained that "bowed" stringed instruments of various capacities are of immense antiquity, and it might be supposed therefore that the basis at least of the modern orchestra had been for centuries past at the disposal of any musician who had genius and enterprise enough to raise that splendid structure upon it. This supposition, however, would be unjust towards the great masters of the Second Period. In comparison with those of later times, the powers of the instruments and of the players upon them were alike insignificant; and these reacted upon each other.

The four forms to which bowed instruments are now restricted were probably all known early in the seventeenth century; but they were lost among a crowd of others, varying, as it would seem, according to the caprice of individual makers or players. The varieties of the *Viol* family, in dimension, shape, number of strings, &c., were very numerous. Specimens enough, not to speak of representations, of these old instruments, have come down to us to enable us to form a fair estimate of their powers. It is quite certain that their intensity and quality of sound (technically, *timbre*) must have been altogether inferior to those of the instruments now in use. An instrument not too large to be held like a violin (*da braccia*), which could bear the weight of eight or ten strings, must have been of too solid a fabric to afford much resonance, or else the strings themselves must have been too thin to make it vibrate to any considerable extent. The same deficiency must have obtained in the graver instruments of the same kind.

On the other hand, the wind instruments, with some exceptions, must have been as much too loud as the stringed were too soft. All modern improvements have gone, not to diminish the possible intensity of wind instruments, but to bring that intensity under control. Thus the horn, now capable of such delicate and various intonation, long bore the name *cor-de-chasse*, which speaks for itself; while the quality both of the oboe and the clarionet has been essentially refined, even in the course of the present century. These two instruments may be regarded as the highly polished descendants of a rustic progenitor—the *calamus* of the eclogue and the "shalm" of the Bible. I am reminded, while dealing with names, of a fact which is not uninteresting, and would be indeed incredible, could anything in respect to the origin or connexion of words be incredible or even surprising to those who have looked into that vast subject. It is that "violin" and "fiddle" are the same, or rather, closely connected words.* The Anglo-Saxon form is *fithele*, which, involving a *th*, became, in Anglo-*Norman* mouths, *fielle*, whence we get easily to *vielle* and *viol*, in Italian *viola*, of which viol*ino* is the diminutive, and viol*one*, the Italian double-bass, the augmentative; violon*cello* being, again, the diminutive of this augmentative, and therefore representing in English a little great-fiddle.

* Diez ("Etymologisches Wörterbuch der Romanishen Sprachen") affiliates these words to the Latin, *vitulari*, to leap like a calf. Certain it is, however, that the bow and the fiddle are (so far as they can be traced) Northern in origin, if not in name. Mr. Chappell has an interesting passage on the subject. See "Popular Music of the Olden Time."

Moreover, the tuning of all keyed instruments was at this time imperfect, and liable to many arbitrary varieties of imperfection. The system of equal temperament, by which all keys or scales are made alike, is not even yet universally accepted; and for ages the vast variety of relations with one another in which musical sounds are of necessity used, was the despair of instrumentalists and instrument makers. An exhaustive history of the contrivances proposed to meet this difficulty would be a large and very interesting book. Examples of them are still presented on old key-boards. The beautiful organ in the Temple Church (built as late as 1687), "in addition to the common number of semitones, possesses an A flat and a D sharp quite distinct from the notes G sharp and E flat."* Similar attempts at what centuries of failure might have shown to be an unattainable and not very necessary perfection, have been and are still being made, even in our own time; but the evils which they propose to cure are so little felt, and the means proposed to cure them would be attended with so much cost and inconvenience, that they add another to the many instances in which "the remedy is worse than the disease."

Of the keyed instruments the noblest, the organ, had attained considerable perfection before the commencement of the Third Period. Even in the fourteenth century there were organists of repute, and of necessity (no performer being so dependent on his instrument) large and fairly appointed organs. In all essentials, the organ may be said to have been perfected about the end of the fifteenth century, when Bernardo Tedesco, a German musician resident at Venice, invented the pedal board, the suggestion even of which, once made, opened out a boundless field of improvement for mechanicians of any skill and ingenuity.

Of the less complicated instruments, every one of which is an

* "The Organ." By Edward Hopkins, p. 448. Cocks, London.

orchestra in itself, the most interesting, the pianoforte, had as yet no existence, save in its embryo, the dulcimer, which is of immense antiquity, and not yet quite extinct. The domestic instruments of the Third Period, as of the Second, were the clavicytherium, the clavichord, the virginal, and the spinet—instruments differing in shape and size, in compass and power, but essentially the same in principle; the tone being produced by some kind of *plectrum* pulling the string out of its place, and setting it in vibration. This class attained perfection in the harpsichord, an instrument on which more than one venerable musician still among us first practised his scales,* but of which specimens become every year more rare. A new harpsichord has not perhaps been made for more than half a century; but clavichords, I believe, are still manufactured in considerable numbers in Germany.

Music for these instruments has always been plentiful enough in every country where they themselves were manufactured and played upon. In Italy, in France, in Germany and in England, composers innumerable, many of whose names and all of whose works are forgotten, laboured then as now to meet that appetite for "some new thing" which, rest assured, is not peculiar to this or any ascertained age. Nor, let me add, is the passion for display, the taste for mere manual dexterity, at all a sudden growth of this nineteenth century, or a necessary consequence of anything essential to the music of the Fourth Period. Music for the virginal and other varieties of the harpsichord family has come down to us which is not merely difficult *for its day*, but difficult for *any* day; demanding for its execution much strength and elasticity and individuality of finger.

Nor were the performers on what we now call orchestral instruments without material on which to exercise their skill.

* Among them, by his own account, the great pianist and composer Ignaz Moscheles (d. 1870).

As vocal music became more difficult of intonation, and more various and intricate in its rhythmical forms, the aid of instrumental accompaniment became first a luxury and afterwards a necessity. And, as the variety of the instruments and the skill of the performers on them increased, instrumental concerted music as distinct from vocal, developed itself from a mere adjunct to a great and independent power.

On Italy still our attention has to be turned to watch the results of this development. To Italy, alike the mother of new arts as the mistress of old, we owe the latest and not the least noble of the forms which it has taken. As the birthplace of inarticulate music, Rome was (even in the seventeenth century) to show herself still "the Eternal City." In 1683 Archangelo Corelli, a native of Imola in the Papal States, being then thirty years of age, published in Rome his first work, a collection of sonatas for two violins and bass, with accompaniment for the organ, or cembalo. It is needless to describe compositions with which every lover of music is more or less familiar; and it would be impertinent to praise that which, at the distance of more than a century and a half, is not merely tolerated but heard with pleasure. The progress of art is not always made on an inclined plane; it is checked from time to time by barriers which present no obvious outlet, and are, to the common eye, inaccessible. Some of the most forbidding of these would seem to have been surmounted by the genius of Corelli. He had certainly few if any models, hardly even a point of departure; he did not so much improve, or correct, or mould, or transform, as create; and his creations were the earliest music, pure and simple, which is still able to give pleasure.

I return now to Carissimi, of the greatest of whose great services to modern music it becomes necessary to speak. He is said to have been the teacher of Alessandro Scarlatti, another example of a musician whose works never by any chance find their way into contemporary concert programmes or domestic portfolios, and whose name even may be heard by some of you now for the first time. Alessandro Scarlatti was, nevertheless, not only an inventive and learned composer, but one of the most popular composers that ever lived. More than that, he was the founder of the Neapolitan School, in which were trained the majority of the greatest musicians of the last century, and which exercised an influence, *in*direct where not direct, on every composer, with probably one exception, who has flourished since. With the school of Naples begins modern musical practice; better methods of fingering keyed instruments, better methods of bowing stringed instruments, and better instruments of all kinds; and, above all these in importance and difficulty, the art of singing.

Three persons of the same family, known as musicians, have borne the name of Scarlatti; Alessandro, Domenico his son, and Giuseppe his grandson. The genius of the founder of the family extended to the second, though not to the third generation. Giuseppe attained the rank of a respectable average musician; but Domenico became the greatest performer of his day on the harpsichord, his compositions for which have had the good fortune to keep a place in public estimation which has been denied to any of the immeasurably superior and far more numerous vocal productions of his father.

Alessandro Scarlatti was born at Trapani, in Sicily, in the year 1659. It is not known how or from whom he learned the elements of his art, but tradition has attributed his instruction in the higher branches of it to Carissimi. Doubts have been thrown on the relationship of these two illustrious musicians, growing out of a comparison of dates. This comparison, however, simply shows that Carissimi must have been very old, and Scarlatti very young, at the time they were master and pupil; no very exceptional case in the history of music. The longevity and the precocity of musicians are alike remarkable; they begin professional life earlier, and end it later, than the majority of other men. Carissimi was, without doubt, living and practising his art in Rome in the year 1672, when he must have been upwards of eighty-five years of age; and there is nothing improbable in the fact of Scarlatti's having received instructions from him for a year or two before this, when he (Scarlatti) would have been at least ten; an age at which many musicians have already attracted attention by their compositions or performance.

Few passages in musical history could be more interesting than this brief intercourse of Carissimi and Scarlatti. Look, for a moment, at the chronological table marked "Italy." At the time of Carissimi's birth the Roman School was in its zenith; its great type, Palestrina, still in the active exercise of his matured powers. Scarlatti lived to know, and to appreciate, Handel. The artistic lives of the two men nearly fill up the hundred and fifty years which I have assigned to the Second Period. Had Scarlatti's career been a little extended, he might have seen Haydn. Palestrina and Haydn! The works of Chaucer and Pope, of Orcagna and Titian, of William of Sens and Sir Christopher Wren, do not present examples of more striking contrast than does the music current when Carissimi entered, and when Scarlatti quitted, the world.

In an early lecture I said that, in tracing the progress of modern music, our attention would have to be directed to four peoples; and first, to the Belgians and French, whom I classed together as one people. The frontier line of France has, in modern times, been so often changed, that it has become very difficult to determine the nationality of more than one illustrious musician. It cannot be denied that the word "Belgian" has been somewhat loosely applied in respect to the great masters of the Second Period; while, on the other hand, the French themselves (who have recently succeeded in adding Columbus, Francis de Sales, and Garibaldi to the list of their compatriots) have never for a moment hesitated to appropriate anybody worth appropriating who, for ever so short a time, had lived under French rule, or borne a Gallicized name. I have therefore spoken always of those great musicians who, whether French or Belgian, are indisputably the founders of modern music, as forming the Gallo-Belgian School. This, you will remember, as an individual school, became extinct, or absorbed into the Italian, in the course of the sixteenth century. Italy, however, proved willing and able to repay with interest her debt both to the Teuton and the Gaul. For the moment we must deal only with the latter.

The history of the French School proper only begins in the second half of the seventeenth century, early in which a charter was granted by Louis XIV. to the Abbé Perrin, Robert Cambert, and the Marquis de Sourdéac, for the presentation, during ten years, of operas and dramas in French verse, after the manner of the Italian. Of this association, the first-named was the poet, the second the composer, and the last the mechanist. During the preparations for turning this charter to account, by the opening of the existing *Académie*, then *Royale* and since by turns *Nationale* and *Impériale*, Perrin and Cambert produced the first veritable French opera, the "Pastorale en Musique," and two others, "Ariane" and "Adonis." The *Académie* was opened (in 1671) with "Pomone," by the same author and composer. This found such favour, that the performances of it occupied the theatre for eight months successively. You may be interested to know the number of persons engaged in the execution of a grand opera in those days, in the best appointed theatre in Europe. The company consisted of five male and four female principal performers, of a chorus of fifteen, and an orchestra of thirteen! The prosperity of the undertaking, despite its privileges and the public support it found, was short-lived, and brought suddenly to an end by the intrigues of a musician, then young but already high in court favour, John Baptiste Lully, born in Florence in 1633.

Lully's early removal to France, his introduction, in a very humble capacity, to the household of Mdlle. de Montpensier, and the accidental discovery of his musical talent by the Comte de Nogent, are facts the most familiar of musical history and biography. There are few musicians about whose life more particulars have been recorded. One thing only is wanting to the completeness of the record—any account of his musical education. He left Italy too young to have profited by the musical instruction of any one of the many excellent teachers with whom that country could have provided him; and musical science and skill were alike non-existent in France at the time when he must have needed most their example and help. Nevertheless he became, if not one of the greatest, one of the most successful composers that has ever lived, and (more extraordinary in a self-taught man) one of the best instrumental performers of his day. He added to these accomplishments that of a talent, above even French average, for comic acting and dancing, great tact in the management of business, and prodigious industry. It is grievous to be obliged to complete his portrait by some very odious traits. Lully was profligate and penurious, insolent and cringing. In all that respects his *personnel*, he may, it is to be hoped, be classed among the "curiosities of musical experience."

The catalogue of Lully's works, if we consider that almost every one of them is a folio volume, is a long one. It is made up of some twenty grand operas ("lyric tragedies" they were then called), of ballets carried on entirely by music, and of "occasional music" in divertissements and other theatrical pieces. The greater portion, if not the whole, of those numerous *entrées de ballets* for which we find directions in the comedies of Molière, were originally Lully's. He wrote also, though not so frequently, for the Church; and his pieces of this kind were mostly on a large scale, both as respects their design and detail.

No operatic music that has yet appeared has enjoyed so long a lease of popularity as the music of Lully,—in France; for it has never obtained even a hearing elsewhere. This popularity was undoubtedly aided by many accidental causes; by the fact, among others, that Lully, being the first modern composer who largely occupied the French ear, was the means, to a great extent, of forming the French taste. He was long compared only with himself, and tried only by canons of his own invention. But his success in France was chiefly due to his dramatic genius, which enabled him to give to the persons of his "lyric tragedies" a musical language fitted to their characters and expressive of the situations in which they were placed. This faculty has always been especially appreciated and cultivated by the French, and to its exercise, in spite of certain conventionalities and peculiarities of French music never quite relished by other nations, the French lyric drama owes its present high position in Europe.

Despite of the adverse criticism of three successive generations—that of Rousseau being neither the least powerful nor the least severe; despite of the advent and acceptance of a new French composer, Rameau; despite of the introduction to the French people of the dramatic music of the Italian schools,—the operas of Lully kept possession of the French stage for more than a century; his "Theseus," the longest lived, having been performed for the last time in the year 1778; one hundred and three years after its first production. Nor was the dynasty of the Lullian race brought to an end ingloriously; its deathblow was dealt by no mean hands. In this same year (1778) were played in Paris the "Armide," "Iphigénie," and "Orphée" of Gluck, the "Roland" and other works of Piccini, and some of the best operas of Anfossi and Paesiello. "Nothing," says a French writer, "short of the sublime inspirations of Gluck, was able to bring to an end this long existence of the works of the old *Surintendant de la Musique de Louis XIV.*

Though, as I have said, the popularity of Lully's music never extended beyond his adopted country, the same remark cannot be applied to the influence of his instruction and example. He formed several pupils, and one of these was an Englishman, whose obligations to his master and whose influence on his contemporaries seem to me to have been hitherto strangely underrated or overlooked.

To understand this we must return to our own country, and see what has happened since we left it. You will remember that, contemporary with the Italian schools of the sixteenth century, there was an English school, not only of great, but of undisputed, excellence. No great change took place in the higher styles of composition, among English musicians, during the first part of the seventeenth century. Orlando Gibbons, whose career was somewhat prematurely interrupted in 1625, exhibits in his writings hardly a trace of the influences, so active and so powerful, which were at work in Italy at this time. He is the last, and to my mind the greatest, of our ancients. The reigns of James I. and of Charles I. (from widely different causes) were neither of them favourable to the cultivation of music. Commonplace workers in the exhausted field of the old tonality were plentiful here as elsewhere; but no musician, to be compared with Carissimi, appeared in England, to work in the vein which Monteverde had opened up. Two men only are in any degree exceptions to this; one of them now utterly unknown even by name, save to the curious; the other only just saved from oblivion by his connexion with the poet Milton. Yet the former was a popular composer of instrumental music fifty years before Corelli published his *Opus Primum;* and the latter—

> First taught our English music how to span
> Words with just note and accent—

nearly half a century before Alessandro Scarlatti entered the world.

I would willingly linger a little over the lives and works of these two interesting persons, John Jenkins and Henry Lawes;* but I have too little time left even to deal with persons of superior claims on your attention. I must pass on at once to the post-Restoration composers; only stopping to remark that, though during the Commonwealth church music was of course never heard and perhaps rarely written and public musical performances of every kind discouraged or prohibited, the musical art appears to have been a good deal cultivated in private.

On the restoration of Charles II., such musicians as were still living, and had not forgotten their art, were drawn from their retreats and placed in positions where their talents might find exercise. Their training, tastes and habits however were of another age. Modern illustrations of the legend of "The Seven Sleepers," they woke up in a world for whose ways they had had no preparation; old-fashioned people, learned in canon and believing in the ecclesiastical modes, called upon to furnish material for the Chapel, and the Chamber Royal,—Charles II. being king.

"His Majesty, who," says an old musical editor, "was a brisk and airy prince, coming to the crown in the flower and vigour of his age, was soon, if I may say so, tired with the grave and solemn way which had been established by Tallis, Byrd, and others, ordered the composers of his chapel to add symphonies, &c., with instruments, to their anthems, and thereupon established a select number of his private musicians to play the symphony and ritornelles which he had appointed. The old masters of music, Dr. Child, Dr. Christopher Gibbons,† and Mr. Low, organists to his Majesty, hardly knew how to

* There is a full account of the former in Roger North's "Memoirs of Music." London, 1846.

† Son of Orlando.

comport themselves with these new-fangled ways, but proceeded in their compositions according to the old style.

"In about four or five years' time, some of the forwardest and brightest children of the Chapel began to be masters of a faculty in composing; this his Majesty greatly encouraged, by indulging their youthful fancies, so that every month at least they produced something new of this kind."

The "children" more particularly alluded to in this extract were Pelham Humphrey, Michael Wise, and John Blow. In the few works which have been preserved of the first of these there seem to me to be indications of genius, unquestionably of taste, of a very high order. Whether the development of a great composer would have been possible, in England, at the time Humphrey was a youth, is a question. In his case assuredly the experiment cannot be said to have been fairly tried. He died (in 1674) at the early age of twenty-seven. Humphrey was sent by Charles II. to Paris, that he might receive instruction from Lully. The direct advantages of his visit were probably limited to frequent hearing of his master's compositions, with now and then a hint from the busy Superintendent about his own The indirect advantages of it are most manifest, not only in his own compositions but in those of his fellow-students Wise and Blow and of their immediate successors in the Chapel Royal, the most distinguished of whom was Henry Purcell.

I remember, when I first became acquainted with the works of Lully, being much astonished to recognise many passages and turns of expression which I had heretofore believed to be the invention of Purcell, whose greater opportunities and possibly greater genius have enabled him to shut out from the view of posterity his immediate predecessors. Humphrey's connexion with Lully explains everything. The passages and turns in question are in no respect indigenous; they may be traced first to Lully, and then in many cases to Carissimi, on whom Lully avowedly formed his style.

In Humphrey's anthem "O Lord my God" is a passage which will at once illustrate my meaning, and give you an opportunity of judging whether my estimate of Humphrey's genius is too high. Many of his modulations and turns of melody have, since his day, been much hackneyed; but they must have been very striking when first heard. The plan of the movement too, if not original, is at least uncommon.

FROM THE ANTHEM "O LORD MY GOD."

PELHAM HUMPHREY.

Fig. 33.

feet I may tell all my bones, They pierc - ed my
hands and my feet, I may tell all my bones.
They stand
They stand star - ing and look - ing up - on me,
star - ing and look-ing up - on me,
And cast lots up - on my ves-ture,
They part my gar-ments among them,

But Humphrey, and every other English composer of his epoch has, as I have said, been eclipsed by the nearer form of Purcell; the musician who has been regarded by all musical historians as the representative of English music, and the type of English composers. Though considerably more extended than that of Humphrey, Purcell's life likewise was a short one. He lived only thirty-seven years; from 1658 to 1695. As with most other great musicians, the powers of Purcell are as remarkable for their variety as for their extent. Specimens of every form practised in his day are to be found in his numerous works; Church Anthems and Services, Latin Motets, Operas, Cantatas, detached Songs, Duets and other vocal pieces, and a prodigious quantity of instrumental music; Sonatas for stringed instruments, and what was then termed Curtain Music, played in theatres between the acts of plays.

Purcell was the first Englishman to demonstrate the possibility of a national opera. His essays of this kind may still be studied with advantage as models; models which unfortunately till of late years, have remained without imitation. No Englishman of the last century succeeded in following Purcell's lead into this domain of art; none indeed would seem even to have understood in what his excellence consisted, or how his success was attained. His dramatic music exhibits the same qualities which had already made the success of Lully; qualities which, near a century later, made the success of Gluck, and in our own time have made that of Meyerbeer,—more or less of musical invention and musical science (as the case may be) but these gifts and acquirements kept in subordination, and exclusively devoted to one object, the carrying on and giving effect to the business of the drama.

For some years after Purcell's death (in 1695) his compositions, of whatever kind, were the chief, if not the only, music heard in England. His reign might have lasted longer, but for the advent of a musician who, though not perhaps more highly gifted, had enjoyed immeasurably greater opportunities of cultivating his gifts, and who (during this Period everything) was born nearly thirty years later.

I speak of George Frederick Handel, so large a portion of whose life was spent in England, and so large a portion of whose works owe their origin to English suggestion, that not only we ourselves but foreigners, hardly excepting even his own countrymen, look upon him as more than half an Englishman.

Whatever good influences we may have had in giving a

direction to Handel's genius, however much he may have owed to his long residence among us, Handel was by birth a German, and by education a citizen of the world. Music (let us never forget it) is a universal language, and Handel had the advantage of studying it wherever, for the time being, it was most and best spoken.

No musical biography is so generally known and so easily accessible as that of Handel. I will not take up your time by the recital of what many of you must know already, but content myself with recalling a few particulars which bear immediately on what I shall have to say about his writings.

He was born in the year 1685, at Halle, in Saxony. Having exhibited the usual precocity of musical genius, he was placed early under the instruction of Zachau, then organist of Halle Cathedral. At the early age of fourteen, the death of his father, a man of whom enough has been recorded to account for some of Handel's subsequent success, threw him on his own resources. He made his way to Hamburg, then at the height of its commercial prosperity, and obtained a place as violinist in the opera orchestra, at that time under the direction of Keiser, one of the greatest musicians then living. In 1705 (ætat. 20) he produced, at Hamburg, his first opera, "Almira," which he followed shortly by three others; these four being the only operas (almost the only works) with German words he ever set. After three years' residence in Hamburg, Handel found himself able to realize the object of every young musician's ambition at this epoch, a visit to Italy.

A glance at the chronological tables will exhibit better than any description, however complete, what temptations the warm South was able to hold out, at the beginning of the last century, to a young Saxon musician more conversant with the necessaries than the luxuries of his art, and who, however conscious of his strength, must have felt and known his weakness in respect to that grace which, when not inborn, is rather a subtle essence to be unconsciously inhaled than matter directly communicable.

At Naples he would find Alessandro Scarlatti in the fullest exercise of his ripened powers, busy with the organization of that great school which sent forth, a little later, Vinci, Leo, Durante, Pergolesi, and the Saxon Hasse; a little later still, Jomelli, Sacchini, Gugliemi; and, more recently, Paesiello and Cimarosa. At Rome he might still catch some of the latest accents of the patriarch of modern instrumental music, Corelli; and study with reverend curiosity those grand musical forms the fleshless skeletons of which still mock the past greatness of the Sistine Chapel. At Venice again he would find one of the most learned and inventive musicians of the Third Period, Antonio Lotti, presiding over the music of the Republic; with fellow labourers like Marcello, Gasparini, and Steffani—who, like Rubens, occasionally *s'amusait d'être ambassadeur.* More than all perhaps to one so thoroughly grounded in the grammar of his art, Handel would hear for the first time the most eminent of those practitioners of what even in Italy was then a new, and everywhere else an unknown art, the art of singing.

To every one of these centres of civilization, however, Handel was rich enough to give something in exchange for what he took away from it. He wrote unceasingly both for the theatre and the chamber. After between two or three years' residence, or more properly locomotion, in Italy, he turned his thoughts and his steps northward; and while deliberating as to which of many offers of permanent homes he should accept, he fell in at the court of the Elector of Hanover (afterwards our George I.), with some English nobleman who induced him to visit this country. Handel arrived in London at the close of 1710 (ætat. 25); and, with the exception of a few flying visits to the Continent, the remainder of his life was spent in England.

No one, musical or unmusical, need be told that Handel

owes his place in the hearts of his countrymen by adoption, to that matchless series of dramas and epics in which he has illustrated the great facts and the great truths of Holy Writ. Yet this series, long as it is, forms but a portion of his entire works, and indeed was the occupation of those years in which most men shrink from new undertakings. Over and above these Oratorios (more than twenty in number), Handel is the composer of a vast number of anthems, psalms, hymns and motets; odes, canticles, duets and trios; of innumerable organ concertos, oboe concertos, harpsichord lessons, concertantes, sonatas, trios, &c. &c., and of some forty operas. Indeed, his introduction to this country was made as an opera composer. For more than a quarter of a century Handel struggled with every kind of difficulty and discouragement in his connexion with the opera stage; never but once attempting the particular form of art in which he was destined at last to make so grand and original a reputation. So long is it sometimes before a man finds out, or the world finds out for him, the particular work which he has been sent into the world to do. To Handel's failure, not as an opera composer but as an opera manager, we owe "Israel in Egypt" and the "Messiah." He attained the ripe age of fifty-three, before he fairly began that new career which has not only given him a place in the first rank of musical inventors but has connected his name with the loftiest and the most important subjects that can occupy the thoughts and move the affections of men.

In the year 1737 Handel's career as an opera manager and as it proved as an opera composer came to an end, so disastrously that even his "iron constitution," hitherto unscathed by toil or trouble, broke down. His mental faculties were temporarily disturbed, and he had an attack of paralysis. A short sojourn at Aix-la-Chapelle, which, greatly against his inclination, he was induced to make, set him up again, so far as to enable him to return to London; and in Lent, 1739, he inaugurated, in the old Haymarket Theatre, a series of performances which from that time he repeated annually. Twenty years more of life and of work were still accorded to him; and twenty years of what noble work! of work how precious in its results to the world! To this epoch we are indebted for the oratorios "Deborah," "Athalia," "Saul," "Israel in Egypt," "Messiah," "Samson," "Joseph," "Hercules," "Belshazzar," the "Occasional Oratorio," "Judas Maccabeus," "Alexander Balus," "Joshua," "Solomon," "Susanna," "Theodora," "Jephtha," and the "Triumph of Time and Truth."

Some of these works are to a great extent either repetitions of one another, or made up of pieces adapted from early compositions, often designed for very different purposes, and cast originally in very different forms. Thus, his collection of "Chamber Duets," published as early as 1711, in Hanover, was called into requisition in the composition of the most esteemed, if not the greatest, of his oratorios, the "Messiah." The choruses, "For unto us a child is born," and "All we like sheep," are based on movements in this collection which had before done duty in "Acis and Galatea" and in "Alexander's Feast," and were still to furnish raw material for "Judas Maccabeus." Moreover, there is no disputing the fact that other people's thoughts, and even their ways of expressing them, as well as his own, found their way into Handel's scores.

That hundreds of subjects, phrases of melody, forms of harmony, points of imitation, sequences, and other musical figures which, having been first introduced to the English public by Handel, are and always will be called "Handelian," are to be found in the works of his Italian predecessors, is indisputable and undisputed. These however are but the "waifs and strays" of music; common property of which it would be hard to find the rightful owner, and therefore best disposed of by annexation to some great estate.

But the charges against Handel do not end here. The noble chorus, "Hear, Jacob's God," in "Samson," is rather a transcript than an imitation of the "Plorate Filiæ Israel," in Carissimi's "Jephtha," from which I gave you an extract just now. The chorus "Egypt was glad at their departing," in "Israel in Egypt," is beyond doubt an adaptation of an organ fugue by a German composer, Kerl, whose works it is certain Handel had studied, while under the instruction of Zachau, at Halle. A claim has been made recently on behalf of Stradella for the outline at least of the chorus in the same oratorio, "He spake the word;" and I suspect, from internal evidence, that a claimant will some day be found for "I will exalt Him."

It is as difficult to believe, as it would be impossible to prove, that these appropriations, quotations, loans, or whatever you like to call them, were made consciously. A man of large possessions may sometimes mistake the boundary line which divides them from those of his neighbours. Certainly, as compared with what is beyond doubt original in Handel's works, these plagiarisms, if such they be, amount to next to nothing. Nor could those from whom they were made reasonably complain of them. Their ideas were attired by him as they had never been before, and presented in companionship such as they could never have found for themselves. For, be the appropriated jewel what it might, Handel in every instance set it so that its owner could not, for wonder and shame, have claimed it for his own. Rather would he have regarded the form in which he found his thought enshrined, as some old martyr or confessor might the reliquary whose workmanship had saved from destruction some atom of his frame, and kept his name in the memory of posterity.

I would willingly dwell a little on the personal character of this great musician and, despite of some failings, good man; on the good and the ill fortune which accompanied his remaining years, the intellectual energy spared to him to the last, and the physical infirmity, loss of sight, of which he "most complained," in notes at least equal in pathos to the words of the great poet who was visited by the same affliction;—but time fails me, and these things have been recorded again and again.

Handel died, in the seventy-fifth year of his age, on the 15th of April, 1759; the day of his death being, as he is recorded to have prayed that it might be, Good Friday.

Were it possible to excite the same interest in the minds of Englishmen in the life and works of any other composer, it would assuredly be in those of his countryman and contemporary, John Sebastian Bach; a man resembling Handel in many particulars, who, by a singular coincidence, was born in the same year (1685), and who, like Handel, though a writer in almost every style practised in his day, owes his fame chiefly to his choral writings. The story of the two lives, however, has no further resemblance. The name Handel represents an individual *sui generis;* that of Bach, if not a species, a race. There is no record of any one of Handel's ancestors or relatives having cultivated, or even cared about, music; his father seems to have despised it. J. S. Bach was one of a fifth generation of a race of musicians tracing back their origin to the beginning of the sixteenth century. Handel left no descendants; Bach was twice married, and became the father of eleven sons and nine daughters. *All* of the former were musicians by profession, and several of them attained to very great eminence. Many of the relatives too of J. S. Bach (uncles, cousins—first, second, and third; once, twice, and thrice removed) were musicians. Up to about the middle of the last century, annual gatherings—veritable *confluentes*—of Bachs were made at Erfurt, Eisenach, or Arnstadt, at which as many as a hundred and twenty of them, all musicians, have been present.

The founder of the Bach family was a baker of Presburg who, driven thence on account of his Protestant opinions, took refuge in the village of Wechmar in Saxe Gotha, and set up as a miller. He was a lover of music and a performer; taste and accomplishment which he succeeded in communicating to and cultivating in two of his sons, John and Christopher. John Sebastian Bach, the grandson of the latter, was born in 1685, at Eisenach. Left an orphan at the age of ten, his elder brother, John Christopher, took charge of him and continued his musical instruction till the time of his own death, when John Sebastian was only fifteen. Thrown entirely on his own resources, he made his way, in company with a schoolfellow, to Luneburg, where both obtained places as choristers in the church of St. Michael, and became students in the Gymnasium. Eager for improvement as a performer on the organ and harpsichord, Bach during his three years' stay at Luneburg twice visited Hamburg to hear the celebrated organist Reincke, then upwards of eighty years of age; and once also the chapel of the Duke of Celle, then chiefly composed of French artists. From Luneburg he proceeded to Weimar, where he became one of the Court musicians. His desire, however, to improve himself continually as an organist soon induced him to become a candidate for the place of one at Arnstadt. This he obtained. Here his vicinity to Lubeck brought him within easy access of Buxtehude, one of the first musicians of his time. To Lubeck he made many pilgrimages, remaining there on one occasion three months, that he might profit by the indirect instruction of its skilful and learned organist; for it does not appear that Bach became his pupil, or even made his acquaintance. At one-and-twenty, Bach was already in considerable repute. Of several positions offered to him, he accepted one at Müllhausen; but at the end of a year, in 1708, during a visit to Weimar, he so charmed the Duke by his performance on the organ, that he made him organist to the Court, and subsequently his concert-master.

On the death of Zachau (Handel's master), his place at Hamburg was offered to Bach. He proceeded thither, and performed in presence of the authorities who had made him the offer; but (why is not recorded) he did not accept it.

In the year 1717, Bach being then thirty-two, Louis Marchand, a Parisian organist of considerable repute, arrived at Dresden and won great admiration at the Court of Augustus by his performances, extemporaneous and other. Volumier, the concert-master, well knowing Bach's powers, and jealous for the honour of his country, invited him to Dresden and made arrangements for a musical "tournament" in which Marchand and Bach were to be the opponents. The former, however, never entered the field; on inquiry it was found that he had quitted Dresden the day before the proposed meeting without taking leave of anybody.* The honours of the occasion of course remained with Bach; for though undisputed, none could deny that they were deservedly his. That Marchand should of his own free will have entered the lists against a champion of such known strength and skill is inconceivable. He was by all account a brilliant and tasteful clavecinist, but his compositions which have come down to us show him to have been a feeble and ill-taught musician.

Shortly after his return to Weimar, Prince Leopold of Anhalt-Cœthen offered him the place of organist and musical director to his chapel. This post he accepted and held during thirteen years; years of peace and happiness during which he was free from those pressing needs and anxieties which, though they often stimulate the productiveness of the artist, as often act injuriously on the quality of what he produces. One of the pleasantest incidents of these pleasant years must have been a second visit he made, in the plenitude of his genius and skill, to Hamburg, to see once again that same Reincke at whose feet he had sat as a youth many years before. This time Bach was the performer, and Reincke, then nearly a hundred years of age (he was born in 1623), the listener. After a sublime

* This story is effectively told in the novel "Friedemann Bach."

extemporization on the choral "An Wasserflussen Babylons," the patriarch exclaimed, "I thought this art was lost, but I see that you have found it."

In 1733 Bach succeeded Kuhnau as "Cantor" or director of the Thomas School of Leipzig, from which town he never migrated, nor indeed, save on one occasion, made even an excursion. This however was an interesting one. In 1740 his second son, Carl Philip Emmanuel, took office under the King of Prussia, Frederick II., at whose desire John Sebastian, accompanied by his eldest son Friedemann, paid a visit to Berlin. It was the king's habit—in the intervals of fighting—to hold concerts every evening, the most striking if not pleasing incidents of which were his own performances on the flute. One of these he was about to begin when, according to custom, the list of strangers who had reached Potsdam in the course of the day was put into his hand. After a glance at this, he turned to the musicians who were waiting to accompany him, and said, "Gentlemen, old Bach is come," and gave orders that the great master should be conducted to the palace forthwith. The king, whose flute was for once silenced for the evening, then proceeded to conduct his travel-stained guest, followed by the entire musical party, through various rooms furnished with pianofortes by Silbermann—a maker for whom some of the earliest improvements in, and even the invention of, the instrument are claimed by his countrymen. On one after another of these Bach played compositions of his own, or extemporized on themes given him by the king or those about him; making them "discourse," as we may well believe, more "excellent music" than they had ever discoursed before.

This was Bach's last journey. The closing years of his life were darkened by the same cloud which overspread those of his great contemporary and only rival, Handel. He recovered his sight suddenly a few days before his death, but was seized with apoplexy almost immediately after. He died on the 30th of

July, 1750, nine years before Handel. Nine years fewer therefore were allotted to him.

During his lifetime, and indeed for many years after his death, Bach's name was far more widely known than were his compositions. Many causes contributed to this. He worked always rather for himself than for others; to relieve an irrepressible productive power rather than to please or, as Handel would have said, to "improve" others. Of his compositions it is probable a vast number were never performed in his hearing; and of those that were, the majority, it is equally probable, were never performed but once. Communication too in the first half of the last century was everywhere difficult. The report of a great work performed in Leipzig might be months in reaching Dresden; the work itself years. Certain it is that in 1788, thirty-eight years after Bach's death, Mozart, in passing through Leipzig, heard for the first time one of his church cantatas. From him, probably acquainted with more music than any musician of his age, its performance called forth the exclamation, "Heaven be praised, here is something new; from this something is to be learnt." No score of the work being accessible, or perhaps extant, he had the separate parts spread out before him, and spent many hours in their study, only interrupted by expressions of wonder and delight at the originality, learning, vigour and beauty of this "new" music.

Since this time Leipzig has been honourably distinguished as pre-eminently the custodian of Bach's reputation. In the Thomas School his works have been, and are still, the object of the most careful study and practice; and it is to Leipzig we owe the projection of the first complete collection of his compositions; a collection which has already reached thirty folio volumes and is still in course of publication.

The influence of Bach's indisputable and undisputed genius has certainly been checked or restricted in its operation by a technical cause; the difficulty, or shall I say ungraciousness, of his vocal writing? To speak of this great musician as wanting in melody, would be to speak of him as wanting in a quality wanting which no musician can be great. But he would seem never to have felt, though he must have known, a very elementary truth; that the voice has peculiarities which take it out of the category of musical instruments "made with hands." In this respect, more perhaps than in any other, he differs from Handel; and the cause of the difference is revealed in the story of the two lives. Handel, at the time when the mind is most apt to receive and to retain impressions, good or bad, travelled into many lands, and so to speak mastered the musical idioms of all Europe. The travels of Bach, like those of the "family of Wakefield," were "from the blue bed to the brown;" he never quitted Germany. Not only so, he would seem to have resisted even the influences brought home to him, which might in some degree have made amends for this. He must have heard, or have had the opportunity of hearing, other than the German singers of his time. Many an Italian Opera Company must have come within his reach. Is it possible that the flimsiness of a good deal of the music sung by a Faustina or a Senesino can have altogether withdrawn his attention from—made him altogether insensible to—the exquisite art with which it was presented? There is a story of Bach, admiringly told by some of his biographers, that at Dresden, where the opera was always open to him, he was wont to say mockingly to his son Friedemann, "Let us go and hear the little songs (*chansonnettes*) of Dresden." If he could only have tolerated those "little songs!" Handel not only tolerated them, but turned his toleration to account, in learning how to write not only what is heard but what is sung with pleasure.

Of no composer so great have such widely different opinions been held as of John Sebastian Bach. There can, of course, be but one opinion as to his science or invention; but in regard to every other qualification of a great musician—sentiment, expression, versatility, taste—opinions vary to the extent of assigning to him, on the one hand, all these in a larger measure than to any other composer, and, on the other, of denying him the possession of a single one of them. Neither of these extreme views can be maintained. J. S. Bach was beyond all question a great and original genius; one of those men born but at rare intervals, and to be reared only in particular conditions of the world. Yet it is impossible to deny that his music is deficient in some element necessary to make it intelligible, and therefore acceptable, to the unlearned hearer. And, wanting this element, whatever it may be, ought any work of art to be regarded as completely great? Should we not at least distrust those works of which artists alone can see the merit? Doubtless to fathom the "deepest deeps" of a great mind requires a plummet that few can handle; but the beauties of form and colour which adorn its surface are not always the worst evidences of its profundity.

That the "Passions Musik" and other cognate works of Bach have hitherto had but a small congregation* in England, proves nothing. The place he might have claimed in our affections was already filled by Handel. But is Bach the Handel even of Germany? Does he enter into the musical life of his countrymen as Handel does into ours? Surely not. Handel's music is an oak which has struck its roots deep into English soil, and spread its "hundred arms so strong" to the sun and the storm of a hundred English summers and winters. Bach's is, so to speak, an exotic, even in Germany; blooming no doubt in the *Conservatorium* and the *Akademie,* but unfit, as yet at least, for open-air life. Whether many specimens of it will ever be acclimatized anywhere remains to be proved.

Be this as it may, some of the productions of this altogether exceptional master will probably outlive all existing music.

* It has largely increased among us since this was written—whether permanently time will show. So indeed has Handel's in Germany.

His forty-eight Fugues which, with as many Preludes, constitute the work originally entitled "Das wohl-temperirte Clavier," are the best examples of their class; and their class is of all others the least susceptible to the influences of popular taste. Fugue is the concentrated essence of what we now call music. It derives nothing from any association with temporal things; it expresses no human emotion, still less does it describe or suggest the actual or even the possible in their relations to ourselves. It has its own aims, and it reaches them in its own way. One can conceive a time—and rejoice in not living in it—when the Preludes to these incomparable productions shall have ceased to have an interest for mankind. That the Fugues which follow them should know the same fortune is inconceivable. It is hard to picture them as having ever been new; harder as ever becoming old. They are Immortals, incognoscent alike of youth or age. We rarely think of a composer, of a *poet*—in the primary or secondary sense of the word—in connexion with them; never that any one of them, given its initiatory *motif*, could be other than what it is—the necessary deductions from a given premiss. They are not so much works of an individual, as things long pre-existent, with which we have somehow been made acquainted. One would as soon think of *criticising* these impersonal, passionless, inevitable entities as of criticising the earth, the air, or the sea. One hesitates equally to apply to or withhold from them the epithets "sublime" or "beautiful;" and the single-minded old Cantor who "found" them would doubtless have wondered at anybody applying either. But they give to those who master them a sense of satisfaction which, viewing the limits of human power, works of different—possibly higher—aim never can give, save to students able to discern, through the obvious and imperfect accomplishment of the artist, his occult and possibly perfect intention.

THE FOURTH PERIOD.

FROM ABOUT A.D. 1750 TO THE PRESENT TIME.

RECAPITULATION—GERMAN COMPOSERS OF THE SECOND PERIOD — SENFL, WALTHER, AND GUMPELZHEIMER—ORGANS AND ORGAN PLAYERS—THE PEDAL-BOARD—THE THIRTY YEARS' WAR—MUSICAL SCIENCE—GERMAN MUSICAL SCHOLARSHIP—DEFICIENCIES—ITALIAN INFLUENCE — OPERA — KEYSER — ITALIAN SINGERS — ITALIAN MUSICAL ACHIEVEMENTS—INSTRUMENTS — INSTRUMENTAL PERFORMANCE—ORATORIO AND OPERA—THE ORCHESTRA—BOWED INSTRUMENTS—THE VIOLIN, VIOLONCELLO, AND DOUBLE BASS — THE OBOE AND BASSOON—THE PIANOFORTE—INSTRUMENTAL MUSIC—BORCHERINI—EMMANUEL BACH—HAYDN—METASTASIO AND PORPORA—HAYDN'S ORATORIOS—THE "SEVEN LAST WORDS"—THE CREATION—"FORM" IN COMPOSITION—MODULATION—ORDER OF KEYS—MOZART—THE MOZART FAMILY—THEIR TRAVELS—THE PRINCE-BISHOP OF SALZBURG—IDOMENEO—DIE ZAUBERFLÖTE—THE REQUIEM

THE FOURTH PERIOD.

We have seen how, in the course of three centuries, music has, so to speak, made the tour of Europe; first Belgium and Northern France, then Italy, and then Germany becoming successively its head-quarters and its home.

It was in the early part of the last century only that Germany began to make for herself a distinct place among the musical nations of Europe; but from about the middle of that century, when the career of J. S. Bach ended, that place has been indisputably the first. In every department of the musical art but one, singing, the German School has equalled, if not surpassed, all others. Even in opera, wherein the element of nationality obtains so largely, Germany has been able to lend two composers, Gluck and Meyerbeer, to the most national of all nations, the French; while under her hands instrumental music has been so unprecedentedly developed, has taken forms so extensive and so various, that she may be fairly said to have opened up a new world to musical Europe.

It would be very much easier to exhibit the progress of music, or indeed the progress of anything, had its steps in all cases been taken at easily ascertained periods, or could they always be attributed to easily ascertained persons. In fact, narrative would be very much less troublesome if the materials for it lay in strata, like the formation of the earth's crust. But events are very indifferent to the convenience of those who have to narrate them; and they frequently compel us to disappoint our hearers, by carrying their thoughts back to times and to facts which have already received what might have been thought their full share of attention.

Thus, with this new world of German art all before us, we must pause for a moment to look back on the old one we are about to leave, and to consider what it has given to this new one we are about to enter.

A glance at the Chronological Table will remind you that from very early times there have been musicians in Germany. Of these the Table does not present anything like a complete catalogue; it does not do so in relation even to Belgium, so important in the Second Period. Long lists of German musicians who flourished in the early part of the sixteenth century appear in the works of native musical historians, who are obliged however to admit that their compositions never, like those of their Belgian contemporaries, found their way into Italy nor, strange to say, attained any success even in the great capitals and courts of Germany. Of these masters Senfl and Walther have been rescued from the catalogue of mere names by their connexion with Luther and the Reformation. In Forkel's "Allgemeine Geschichte der Musik,"* among other contemporary native works, is a composition by Stephen Mahu which gives a high idea of the science and (what in his day was much more rare) even the taste of that master. It is written in five parts, in a grandiose and flowing style, and might be termed a *motet*, but that it is set to some words evidently intended to be humorous but of which the humour is not very obvious.

Towards the end of the sixteenth century, again, appear the names of other musicians whose works attained not much circulation even in Germany, and none elsewhere. Attention has lately been drawn to one of these, Gumpelzheimer, by a distinguished French critic, M. Fétis, who speaks of him as a

* Vol. ii. p. 686.

composer far in advance of his contemporaries, and whose works even present examples of some of the effects claimed as the subsequent invention of Monteverde. It is singular that Gumpelzheimer's compositions, many of them in print, should have been before the world for nearly three centuries without ever having excited like notice or admiration till now.

These and other musicians, however, if not men of genius, were at least men of culture, cognisant of the theory, and well trained in the practice of their art—of one branch of the latter especially, and that requiring, beyond all others, the profoundest acquaintance with, and the readiest use of all the resources of, musical science, *organ-playing*. Germany has long been pre-eminently the land of organs and of organ-players. Of the two greatest advances possible in the instrument itself, the formation of the finger-board and the addition of pedals, the latter certainly, as has been already shown, was the invention of a German, known as Bernardo Tedesco. Much as this noble instrument has been improved in modern times, especially in those nearest to us, no improvement has been made, perhaps none could be made, to be compared in importance with that of Bernardo. For the inventor of pedals, in adding to the resources of the performer, added to the resources of music; calling into existence of necessity notes of depth and volume unknown before.

Strange to say, the German School of Music does not seem to have been seriously affected even by the intense and protracted misery brought on Germany by the Thirty Years' War. The acts of that fearful tragedy range from the year 1618 to the middle of the seventeenth century; and it was during those and the years immediately following, that innumerable musicians about whose ability there can be no reasonable doubt (among them were the teachers of Handel and Bach) received their education. No reader of history need be told that times of political perturbation have been mostly favourable to the production of men of genius. In such times public events follow one another with unusual rapidity, private life becomes more varied and adventurous, and the imagination is nourished from a thousand sources which are closed to it when things take their ordinary course. But it is altogether exceptional, surely, to find a country emerging from a struggle which cost her, according to some historians, two-thirds of her population, with a large staff—not of inventive, undisciplined musicians of genius, but—of uninventive, well-informed, well-trained contrapuntists. That such was the case in Germany after the Thirty Years' War is certain; and nothing could have been more fortunate, so far as the modern German school was concerned. To this cause, in a very great degree at least, must the pre-eminence of that school be attributed. The English composers of the sixteenth century, as we have already seen, rivalled in number and in excellence even their Italian contemporaries. Those of Germany hold no place beside them. Yet our civil wars of the seventeenth century, followed by the Commonwealth, annihilated the old English school of music, and left the post-Restoration composers with that "too much liberty," the weight of which impedes the action of the most original minds. That Pelham Humphrey, Blow, and more especially Purcell, were persons richly endowed by nature with musical genius, is certain; and that the evidence of this genius is to be sought in their intention rather than their execution, is as much so.

And here I cannot refrain from pressing on your attention a fact, in respect to music, not often noticed, and more rarely appreciated,—that no lasting musical reputation has been erected on any but a deep and solid foundation of musical science. The shallowest and least-instructed hearer soon loses his interest in an ill-constructed composition. A well-constructed composition may be dull; every scholar is not a man of genius. But an ill-constructed one induces something worse than weariness, disgust.

The most popular composers the world has yet seen have been also the most learned; and the decline in reputation of many a man of genius is due, not so much to change of fashion or improvement in the resources of his art since he practised it, as to some deficiency in his training, put out for a moment even from his own sight by the brilliancy of his invention.

If I add that the most original works of every great musician have been produced towards the close of his career, let his career have been long or short, I shall only confirm my assertion that the music most pleasing, even to the common auditor, is also the most scientific.

The German musicians of the Second, and the first years of the Third, Period exhibited little, perhaps no, genius or individuality; but they were, I repeat, musicians—scholars in music. And the traditions of their scholarship were unbroken, even by the Thirty Years' War. J. Amboise Bach, the father of J. *Sebastian* Bach, was an accomplished musician; so were his grandfather J. Christopher, and his great-grandfather Hans Bach. Handel's master, Zachau, was but an average example of a very numerous body of thoroughly well-trained masters of the musical art and science of their day. Such men make the best of teachers; and it is only when original genius has had the advantage of the severe discipline, the sobering influence, which they are able to bring to bear upon it, that it has escaped the perils which always threaten, and the disgraces which so often have overtaken, it.

Science however, it need not be said, will not make a complete artist; not even with invention superadded to it. There is a grace "beyond the reach of art," but with which art must somehow become imbued, in the absence of which the most original and well-ordered ideas will be wanting in charm, and will fail in obtaining acceptance with the world. Doubtless the business of a great artist is to touch the heart; but he can only get at the heart through the ear or the eye; fastidious members, which do not take easily to those whose appearance is against them.

The German School of the seventeenth century was, to a great extent, wanting in this grace; and there is every likelihood that it would have continued to want it till now, but for the Italians. Look again at the Chronological Table. Of the German composers of the eighteenth century whose names you see there, and of many others of less note whose names are omitted, the majority were directly affected by Italian teaching and Italian example. Of Handel I have already spoken. Hasse, whose deficiencies were revealed to him by the very means which would have concealed them from an inferior man, the production of a *successful* opera, set off immediately afterwards for Italy, where he remained seven years; long enough indeed to acquire an Italian sobriquet, "Il Sassone." Graun, his contemporary, and like him a singer as well as a composer, owed the foundation of his style to the happy accident of a residence in early life at Dresden, where he had frequent opportunities of hearing the operas of the Venetian Lotti, performed by Tesi, Senesino, and other Italian singers. Gluck, of whom more hereafter, spent four years of his early manhood in Italy. So with many others.

On the other hand, both the Scarlattis, father and son, spent many years in Germany, whither indeed most of the pupils of the School of Naples, founded, you will remember, by the former, made their way at some time of their lives. Of these the most influential, perhaps, was Nicolo Porpora, the best years of whose long and laborious life were passed in Germany. He had the honour, as we shall see presently, to become one of the teachers of Joseph Haydn.

Up to the close of the last century the only operas performed in Germany were the works of Italians or, in some few instances, operas in the Italian language, set by German composers (Winter, for example) who strove in every way to form themselves on the Italian model. The majority of the works of Graun are Italian operas, in which he himself, like his contemporary Hasse, acted and sung. The greater part of Handel's life, you will remember, was spent in the setting of Italian opera books; and he came to England avowedly as an "eminent Italian master," a designation often applied to him at the time. The only thoroughly German opera composer worthy especial mention belongs to an earlier epoch than that of which I am now speaking. This was Reinhard Keyser, a man doubtless of great genius and even greater industry. He is said to have produced no less than a hundred and eighteen musical dramas, besides innumerable divertissements, serenades, cantatas, and other pieces. He combined with the occupation afforded by the composition of these, the office (never a *sinecure*) of Managing Director of the Opera-house at Hamburg. Assuredly as his operas were shorter, so his opera singers must have been more manageable, than those of later times. Keyser's school died with him. Gluck, who might have breathed new life into it, was as unresisting to the influence of Italian taste, in the early part of his career, as the most commonplace of his contemporaries.

But perhaps the recent music of northern Europe owes more of its fancy and refinement to the influence of the singers, than even of the composers, of Italy. No form of the musical art has such charm for learned and unlearned; none appeals to so large a public; none exercises the same amount of influence—influence not confined to musical practice, but reacting, usefully and gratefully, on that to which it owes its existence, composition. The last century is pre-eminently the age of great Italian singers. The name of more than one has come down to us from the preceding century; more especially that of Stradella, whose romantic story is perhaps more widely known than anything else in musical history. Stradella, however, was also a composer of great merit, and should be regarded rather as a modern representative of the old *Trouvère* than as a mere singer, in our sense of the term. There have been singers, doubtless, time immemorial. A beautiful voice giving expression to real sentiment is, in a certain sense, singing. But the art first taught in the schools of Italy, about the end of the seventeenth century, was something as much greater than this as the whole is greater than its part.

The achievements of the modern German school are so numerous, so splendid and, more than all, so recent, that those even who are most familiar with musical history reckon up, with a kind of unwilling surprise, the obligations of that school to the Italian; and those who know nothing of musical history are absolutely incredulous as to the extent of those obligations. Let us see what they amount to.

(1.) The Italians are the inventors of some, and the perfecters or at least improvers of most, of the instruments used in the modern orchestra.

(2.) The resources of these instruments were first developed in Italy, and the earliest great performers on them were Italians.

(3.) Not only were the Oratorio and the Opera born and bred in Italy, but every distinct form of musical composition, instrumental as well as vocal, is the invention of Italians.

The demonstration of this will not take us long.

(1.) Instrumental performance is only possible and tolerable under certain conditions. Without approximate mechanical perfection its means and appliances are useless, or worse than useless; from instruments of music they become instruments of torture. In respect to a great and complex machine like an organ, with its multitudinous array of pipes, pallets, feeders, and trackers—its animal, vegetable, and mineral being—this will be obvious. It will be within everybody's experience or observation too that even a pianoforte, so much less intricate than an organ, is useless unless it will keep in tune a reasonable time, and answer always to the touch. But it is not so evident that a performer on the violin or violoncello, comparatively so simple in form and construction, is just as much at the mercy of *his* instrument. Yet this is certainly the case. The proverb, "Good workmen do not quarrel with their tools," has no application to musical performance.

Without perfect instruments perfect execution is impossible; and, failing this, instrumental music itself could never have reached any high degree of excellence. The judicious composer will abstain from demanding impossibilities of his executants, but he is justified in taxing their skill to the utmost, when the utmost skill is needed for the interpretation of his thoughts.

An average full orchestra consists (1) of violins, violas, violoncellos, and double-basses; and (2) of flutes, oboes, clarionets, bassoons, horns, trumpets, trombones, and kettle-drums. Other instruments are, exceptionally, added. Of these instruments, the first-named class outnumbers the others greatly. We rarely, for instance, admit more than two flutes, two oboes, two clarionets, or two bassoons, into the same orchestra; and we frequently have as many as twenty-four violins, eight violas, and as many violoncellos and double-basses;—in all, fifty stringed instruments. Till the beginning of the Fourth Period the orchestra consisted chiefly, and often wholly, of this latter class. Its importance is still paramount.

The undoubted ignorance of the cultivated nations of antiquity of bowed instruments, is one of the strongest arguments against the possibility of their having had anything worthy to be called orchestral music. That the bow is a very ancient invention is now ascertained beyond doubt; but it was long used only by very rude nations, and its latent powers have only been recognised in modern times, and developed quite recently. The viols of our ancestors, even of the seventeenth century, were, it is certain, utterly inadequate to the force, rapidity and, above all, expression attainable through modern stringed instruments,—without which, I repeat, modern instrumental music could not be performed, and would, therefore, never have been written.

The rapid development of the viol family into the viola, violino, violone (or contrabasso), and violoncello, may be fairly called an invention, and an invention the honour of which is due to the Italians. That of the violin has been claimed for, or rather *by*, the French, on, I believe, one single plea; that in some early Italian scores (*e.g.*, Monteverde's *Orfeo*) are found the words "Piccoli violini alla Francese." There is good reason for believing that these "Piccoli violini" were instruments analogous to the "kits" used to this day by dancing-masters. But granting them to have been violins proper, their appearance in Monteverde's score, published as late as 1615, proves nothing. Vincenzo Galilei asserts in his "Dialogues" (printed at Venice in 1568), that the violino and the violoncello were both invented by the Neapolitans. Montaigne has recorded that he heard violins in the great church (St. Zeno?) at Verona, in 1578. Corelli possessed a violin which had been decorated by the Bolognese painter Annibale Caracci, who *died* in 1609; and, to complete the case of the Italians, the first great *performer* on the violin of whom we have any account was an Italian, Baltazarini, who was brought or sent for into France by Catherine de' Medici, in 1577. No specimen of a French violin, no record of a French violinist, has come down to us of anything like these early dates. The invention of the violoncello, again, has been claimed on behalf of a certain Abbé Tardieu, of Provence, who lived in the beginning of the last century. It is certain, however, that Battistini, a Florentine, had brought the instrument into France at the end of the preceding century. Specimens both of the violoncello and of the contrabasso, of Italian fabrication of the beginning of the seventeenth century, are not rare. A representation of one of the latter appears in the well-known picture of Paul Veronese, "The Marriage at Cana," painted *c.* 1660. The figure in the foreground, near the centre (a portrait of Titian), plays upon it.

I may add that the present form of bow used for the violin, viola, and violoncello is the invention of Viotti, that for the double-bass, of Dragonetti; both Italians.

The origin of the reed, like that of the bow, is lost in antiquity: the oboe, however, was greatly improved about the end of the last century by the brothers Besozzi, natives of Parma. The bassoon is the invention of a Canon of Pavia, Afranio, dating as early as 1539.

So much for the orchestral instruments. The catalogue of Italian inventions is not yet, however, exhausted; for I have to add to it one more interesting perhaps than any to which I have yet referred—that of the pianoforte, which was invented by Bartolomeo Cristofali, a native of Padua, about the year 1710. The priority of his claim, not uncontested, has been established beyond doubt by an article in the "Giornale dei Litterati d'Italia,"* written by the celebrated antiquary Scipione Maffei.†

(2.) As might be expected, the first great performers on these instruments were compatriots of their first great factors. I might add that the line has been unbroken, and that the last, as well as the first, eminent performers on most of them have been Italians. We have seen Baltazarini in France, in the sixteenth century. A little later we hear of Bassani, the teacher of Corelli, then of Corelli's pupil Geminiani; of Tartini, renowned also for his discoveries in acoustics, of Giardini and Viotti; and later still, in our own day, of Paganini. Not to multiply instances, in the last century the most eminent players on the violoncello, were the Cervettos, father and son; while the powers of the contrabasso owe their development to a

* Vol. v. p. 144.

† See "The Pianoforte, its Origin," &c. By Edw. Rimbault. Chap. vii.

musician only recently taken from among us, Dragonetti, whom doubtless many here present remember perfectly well.

(3.) For these instruments, singly or combined, every description of music was first written by Italians.

The earliest quartet for stringed instruments of which we have any account, was the work of Gregorio Allegri who died in 1652. The trios and concertos of Corelli, which range from 1683 to 1713, present the only examples of instrumental music of this date which is still able to give pleasure. Without disparagement to the claims of Hadyn as an inventor, it must be admitted that his Italian contemporary, Boccherini, published excellent chamber music, which attained great circulation, while Hadyn was still comparatively unknown.

The invention of the overture is generally attributed to J. B. Lully, whose life and works were assuredly French, but who was born at Florence.

The earliest writer for the keyed instruments which preceded the pianoforte, who attained European fame, was Frescobaldi, a native of Ferrara, whose first publication is dated 1615. The most distinguished of the founders of the modern pianoforte school was Clementi, whose long residence in our own country does not alter the fact that he was born (in 1755) at Rome.

I need not repeat that unaccompanied vocal music attained high perfection in Italy even in the sixteenth century, and that all those grand forms which result from the combination of instruments with voices were at least outlined by Italian hands. The names oratorio, opera (seria e buffa), cantata, serenata—I will not add to the list—tell their own story and proclaim their origin.

If, then, we consider the relative conditions of Italian and German music in the first half of the last century, our surprise at the influence of the former on the latter will be considerably lessened. Musical Germany was in the only condition which can enable a nation or an individual to derive advantage from association with its elders. It had natural strength developed by a certain amount of judicious training—energy, freshness, aptitude. It lacked refinement, ease, grace—all those products of old civilization in which Italy had become so rich. To know these was to appreciate them; and once appreciated they were easy to turn to account in new directions and in new forms. The results of this achievement were first completely exhibited in the works of Joseph Haydn. Not but that very meritorious attempts at grafting Italian sweetness on German strength had been made by his predecessors. To one of them especially modern music owes a large debt of gratitude. From no account of this, however rapid or however slight, should the name of Carl Philip Emmanuel Bach be omitted. This composer, sometimes called Bach of Berlin, was the second son of the great John Sebastian Bach. To say that he was his father's pupil is to say that he was well instructed in all the musical science of his time. He was a youth when the flood of Italian art spread over Germany was still rising. It has left its impress on his works which, without ceasing to be national or individual, have an ease and sweetness that only southern sympathies could have given them. After some years of comparative neglect, attention has recently been recalled to this very elegant writer, whose pianoforte or, more properly, clavichord music* is within the reach of very moderate mechanical powers. There are two beautiful specimens of it in Dr. Rimbault's "Origin of the Pianoforte;" and a small collection has recently been published in Paris, edited by M. Fétis.

* In an interesting account of a visit to C. P. Emmanuel Bach, Dr. Burney says, "In the pathetic and slow movements, wherever he had a long note to express, he absolutely contrived to produce, from his instrument, a cry of sorrow and complaint, such as can only be effected upon the clavichord, and perhaps by himself."—"Present State of Music in Germany," vol. ii. 270.

I must return, however, to Haydn, whose epoch—for it includes that of Mozart—demands all the time and attention we have to spare for it.

Of the facts of Haydn's outer life, which are accessible in many popular forms, I shall content myself with mentioning that he was born at Rohrau, near Vienna, in 1732, and that his first instructor was his father, who combined with the trade of a wheelwright the somewhat incompatible professions of magistrate, sacristan, and organist. As a child he was brought early under the notice of Reüter, Chapel-master of St. Stephen's, Vienna, in the choir of which he remained till the loss of his (treble) voice threw him on the world without friends or calling; his sole possessions a worm-eaten clavecin, two treatises on the theory of music (the "Gradus ad Parnassum" of Fux, and the "Vollkomene Kapellmeister" of Mattheson), and the first six sonatas of C. P. Emmanuel Bach. A very poor hair-dresser named Keller—his name deserves to be recorded—who had formerly admired Haydn's singing when he had a voice, offered him a home and a garret *au sixième,* in which, having installed himself, he set to work, unaided, to fathom the mysteries of harmony and counterpoint, and to make himself a clavecinist. After a time, a few engagements just prevented his being a burden to his good host, the locality of whose dwelling had a singular influence on Haydn's fortunes. In the same *hôtel* lived the poet Metastasio, through whose introduction he was made known to the Venetian ambassador, in whose service was the eminent composer and singing-master Porpora, at this time upwards of seventy years of age.

Perhaps it would have been impossible to have found, in all Europe, two persons more likely to be of use at this time to a young German musician of genius, industry, and modesty such as Haydn's, than Metastasio and Porpora. Though not a profound musician, Metastasio possessed considerable knowledge of the art; and the particular direction his poetical genius had taken, and his manner of life, must have made him one of the best of musical critics. Porpora, on the other hand, was steeped in the musical science of his time, and his taste, both in music and in musical execution, had been formed and polished by long familiarity with the finest models.

The counsels of Metastasio were given with unhesitating kindness; but those of Porpora had to be earned by somewhat humiliating services, and the endurance of continual ill-humour. During a visit he made, in the ambassador's suite, to the baths of Mauensdorf, Haydn descended every morning to the old Maestro's room, brushed his clothes, cleaned his shoes, and powdered his wig,—not pleasant offices for the young artist, but amply indemnified to him by some precious bit of knowledge or morsel of criticism thrown at, rather than given to him, from time to time, in part payment for them. Haydn's amiability and aptitude, however, at length found their way to some weak place in old Porpora's heart, and fairly opened the stores of his learning to his volunteer *valet de chambre.* How long he enjoyed the advantage of these instructions has not been recorded. Porpora is supposed to have died about the year 1758, when Haydn must have been four-and-twenty. From about this time, almost to the day of his death, a period of fifty years, Haydn continued without intermission the exercise of his invention; letting no day pass without a line, and growing from year to year in skill, facility, and reputation.

The number of his compositions is said to amount to about eight hundred. Some of these were, of course, short if not slight productions; but not a few are works of great extent and high finish. For example, Haydn is the composer of four oratorios, of twenty-two operas, of nineteen masses, of eighty-three instrumental quartets, and of a hundred and eighteen orchestral symphonies. Many of his minor works have perished. While in the service of the Prince Nicolas Esterhazy he wrote a hundred and sixty-three pieces for the baryton, an instrument of the now extinct family of viols, on which the Prince was a performer. Nearly all of these were destroyed by fire. It would be unreasonable, however, to regard their composition as lost labour. The process must have added to the composer's facility of expression; and it is probable, as in the case of Handel, that many ideas first called into existence in connexion with these *pièces de circonstance,* were afterwards reproduced, in more developed and more permanent forms. Some of Haydn's greater works too maintain their places only in the libraries of the curious, and are disturbed only at rare intervals. It may be safe to say, that no one of his operas will ever be performed entire again. But, all these compositions deducted, there remains, of the work of Haydn, a quantity alike amazing for its amount, and precious for its invention, science, and beauty.

Of his oratorios, "The Return of Tobias," "The Seven Last Words," "The Creation," and "The Seasons," the second is, perhaps, that which displays the greatest genius, as the third is, beyond doubt, the most popular. "The Seven Last Words" was, in its original form, a purely instrumental work; a series of symphonies intended to follow immediately on as many short sermons on each of the sentences uttered by our Lord on the cross. The text was added subsequently, it is said, by Haydn's younger brother, Michael. It therefore in no way answers to the common conditions of an oratorio, and might, with more propriety, be called, like some of Bach's works, "Passions Musik." Some of the individual movements of this work have, perhaps, never been surpassed, in respect whether to sweetness or energy. They abound in passages which have since become very common, but which no repetition out of their place can make less interesting in it—Haydn's score. But the genius of the composer can only be fully estimated by regarding the work as a whole, and in this respect it is, I believe, altogether unique; a succession of nine unconnected movements, all *Adagios,* but so various in their subjects and treatment, that they have nothing in common but their solemn pace and their unspeakable beauty.

Who shall undertake to say anything that has not been said before, in praise of the "Creation"?—of its fresh and lovely songs, its bright choruses, its picturesque recitatives?—of the variety and felicity of its instrumentation? If the English of the last century were not very productive of fine music themselves, they were certainly the cause of productiveness in others. The "Creation" owes its origin to a visit made by Haydn, in 1791, to London, where he first heard some of the oratorios of Handel—themselves English inspirations. These mighty works were scarcely known, even by name, and assuredly had never been heard, in Germany, up to this time. It would be easy to imagine the impression they must have made on Haydn, had we no evidence of it in the result, which was the production of something of the same class, but altogether unlike them in kind. The modesty, judgment, and, let me add, the self-respect of Haydn, show themselves to great advantage in this circumstance. A man morally and musically inferior would have tried to do something like that which he admired, as the frog tried to be an ox; and he would have failed, respectably or ridiculously, as the case might be, but inevitably. Haydn set to work to do his best, in his own way; and the result was not a second-hand, and of necessity second-rate, "Israel in Egypt," but a "Creation"—so different from the works which had suggested it, that comparison between it and them would be absurd or impossible.

To bring out at all fully the obligations of modern music to Haydn, it is necessary to enter for a moment on a matter of musical technicality—plan, or form, in composition. By either of these terms is generally understood the order in which the musical ideas (*motifs*) of a movement are presented and developed; and, in necessary connexion with this, the succession of scales or keys into and out of which the music passes in its course.

I have already called your attention to the fact that musical composition involves—I might say, means—the presentation of one or more passages at not unfrequent intervals, and under different circumstances.

Now, the old masters practised this art of presenting a given musical figure in different lights, to borrow an expression from another art, with much skill; and, from a fancied analogy which explains itself, they called the passage of a subject in and out of the various parts of a movement, "fugue;" from *fuga*, flight. But the nature of the old tonality forbade the systematic modulation which is one of the conditions of modern musical form. Indeed, modulation, in our sense of the word, was with them impossible; for no two of the old scales were precisely alike. Their modulation only survives in our change of mode, from the major to the minor, and *vice versâ*. All modern scales, in the same mode, are alike; and not only so, but every modern scale is intimately connected with several others.

Thus the scales of C, G, and F have five notes, C, D, E, G, and A, common to all three; B being natural in the scale of C, and flat in that of F; and F being natural in the scale of C, and sharp in that of G. Moreover, the chord of C is common to all three scales: it is the tonic of C, the dominant of F, and the sub-dominant of G. (See *, Figs. 34, 35, and 36.)

Fig. 34.

Fig. 35.

Fig. 36.

Modulation therefore, among scales thus related, would be one of the first things suggested by their use; but it has been reserved for modern musicians to discover, and to settle, the *order* which such modulation should take in an entire movement.

The easiest and most simple and obvious modulation is made by adding a minor seventh to any individual tonic chord, which thus instantly becomes the dominant of a scale requiring a flat more or a sharp less.

Fig. 37.

Such modulation, however, is like rolling down hill, which entails the penalty of climbing up again; it is *too* "easy, and simple, and obvious," for introduction at the beginning of a composition, and is usually reserved till a point has been reached whence it may be made with safety. In fact, the very reverse process is that adopted by modern composers, which is to make their way as soon as possible to a scale or key having a sharp more, or a flat less, than the original scale, and to give out their subject or subjects for the first time in the scale of its dominant. For instance, if a movement begins in C, the aim of the modern composer will be to get soon into G; then to give out his subject or subjects in that key, and after certain episodes, in which these subjects will probably play some part, to repeat them in the key in which he originally started, that of C. The consistency of this succession of keys with their natural relations one to another, and with innumerable facts explicable by the science of harmony, is incontestable; and the form which is the result of its observance is so gratifying to the ear, and so satisfactory to the musical sense, that it has never yet been abandoned by any composer who had once learnt how to work in it. Of course, there are many ways of doing this; and every composer of genius has a way of his own. But examine for yourselves the first movement, in which it is generally most clearly traceable, of any sonata, symphony, or quartet, or the *allegro* of any overture by any modern master of repute, and you will find it constructed on this plan; or, if it be in a minor key, on a somewhat different plan, having a similar "basis in nature."

Now, it cannot be pretended that Haydn, or any other individual composer, invented this form. It was the necessary complement of modern tonality, the result of many an unsuccessful experiment, the tardy fruit of a long course of cultivation. But Haydn was the first man of great genius who appreciated it thoroughly; and some of the first beautiful music in which its influence is clearly perceptible was from his pen.

It is a fortunate and convenient circumstance for me that the greater, the more recent, and the more popular a composer may be, the less necessity there is for my saying very much about him. As you have seen, I have striven to awaken your interest in more than one great musician who I might reasonably suppose was, from his date or the inaccessibility of his works, a mere name to you, if so much. But the lives of the great modern masters are easily accessible; and their works are, in this great age, and (let me say) this great country, of musical performance, living things. Otherwise, I might indeed shrink from mentioning, at the close of a lecture like this, even the name of Mozart.

I shall confine myself to the mention of a few dates which may perhaps enable you to estimate him more justly, and therefore more highly, if that be possible, than you have hitherto done, and to a few facts which will in some degree account for some of his unprecedented and possibly still unequalled greatness.

First, you will notice his position chronologically in reference to Haydn; that he was born, in 1756, twenty-four years after Haydn, but that Haydn survived him no less than eighteen years: the career of Haydn being extended to seventy-seven years, that of Mozart limited to thirty-five, less than half the number. The obligations of Mozart to Haydn, Mozart himself was always the first to acknowledge; those of Haydn to Mozart, though equally admitted by the elder musician, have not been quite so readily understood, or so freely acknowledged by the world. Yet could nothing be more easy of demonstration. The majority of Haydn's greatest works were written *after the death of Mozart.* Of Haydn's twelve grand symphonies (known as the Saloman set), six were composed in 1791, the year in which Mozart died, and the remaining six two years after, in 1793. The "Creation," only begun in 1795, was not finished till 1798. The "Seasons" was of still later date, the last great musical work of the eighteenth century.

If Mozart was, as I think he was, the greatest musical genius the world had yet seen, the circumstances of his birth and early training were the best fitted to develope that genius that could possibly be conceived. If there was never such a pupil as Mozart, surely there was never such a teacher as Mozart's father,—an admirable musician, and a man richly endowed with that precious commodity, common sense; who at the earliest possible moment appreciated the wonderful faculties of his son; and who, from that moment, made their culture the one object and business of his life. Musical prodigies are by no means rare, but the instances in which they have ripened into great or even good musicians are but few. We should not perhaps have been talking about Mozart just now, but for the teaching of his learned, judicious and self-denying father. Moreover, Mozart had the additional advantage of a companion in his studies, a sister, five years his senior, who, as a child, showed hardly less promise than he.

It must be admitted, however, that these inestimable advantages were brought to bear on a subject singularly apt to profit by them. All juvenile prodigies sink into insignificance in comparison with Mozart. Instances without number have been recorded of children whose happy organization enabled them to do with ease what many a well-trained artist does with difficulty,—analyse any number of simultaneous sounds, or recognise any individual one; detect mistakes in the performance of the most intricate and elaborate music; and so on. But Mozart played the clavecin in the presence of innumerable witnesses at the age of four, and between that age and six dictated to his father a number of minuets and other little pieces, some of which have been preserved. At the age of six he played a concerto at Munich, in the presence of the then Elector of Bavaria, and in the same year at Vienna, in that of the Emperor Francis I. At seven he astounded a party of musicians, including his own father, who had never lost sight of him for a single day, by taking part, at sight, in a trio for stringed instruments; having never received a lesson on the violin, nor had any practice save on a small one which had been given to him as a plaything.

In the year 1763 Mozart, being then nine, was taken to Paris, where his first publications, two sonatas for the clavecin, were made known; and in the following year the Mozart family visited London, where they resided fifteen months; Wolfgang exciting always and everywhere the same admiration. On their way back to Salzburg they appeared at the principal cities of the Netherlands; at one of which, the Hague, both the children were brought to the very brink of the grave by a malignant fever. Restored at last to health, they made a second visit to Paris, and finally returned, through Switzerland, to Salzburg, after an absence of three years.

Mozart's visit to London, like Haydn's, made some thirty years later, had a most important effect on his subsequent career. He there became acquainted with the works of Handel, then only recently dead, which were of course objects of veneration in England almost amounting to idolatry. He is said to have taken copies of many of these back to Salzburg, and, together with some of the instrumental works of C. P. Emmanuel Bach, then in the zenith of his fame, to have made them subjects of the closest study. The Mozart family remained for some time in their native city; and during this, almost the only period of tranquillity Wolfgang ever enjoyed, he made acquaintance with some of the best works of the Italian masters of the sixteenth century.

In 1767 the family set out again on another journey, to Vienna. Here, having played in the presence of the Emperor Joseph II., he made, by imperial desire, his first attempt at dramatic composition in "La Finta Semplice." During this journey both he and his sister had a second narrow escape; this time from smallpox, of so serious a character that the boy lost his sight from the effects of it for nine days. On his return to Salzburg, at the end of 1768, he applied himself diligently again to his studies for a year, during which he learned the Italian language. This accomplishment was made with an especial object. In the last days of 1769 his father and he, without his sister, set off on a journey into Italy. They visited Verona, Mantua, Milan, Florence, Rome, and Naples. The majority of the first generation of great masters of the Neapolitan School had, at this time (1769), been gathered to their fathers: the second were in the full exercise of their ripened powers; more often, as I have already shown, abroad than at home. But the works of the former were still current; and every church, academy, and theatre echoed to the strains of a Scarlatti, a Leo, a Durante, or a Pergolesi.

Mozart, however, like Handel, who had trodden the same road more than half a century earlier (in 1706–9), could pay back even the Italians of this epoch in their own coin. He was received everywhere with enthusiasm, such enthusiasm as is never exhibited save among Transalpine people. Poems were written, medals were struck, in his honour; academies opened their doors to him; and the most learned and skilled musicians did amazed homage to a youth of fourteen who played the most intricate compositions at sight, with a force and delicacy altogether without precedent or parallel; who poured forth extemporaneously magnificent music in every style, from a fugue on three subjects to a one-fingered waltz; who built motets on a plain song like a Roman of the sixteenth century; and who wrote concertos, sonatas, fantasias, and capriccios, as none had written before him.

In 1772 the Mozarts, father and son, were recalled to Salzburg by the installation of a new Prince-Bishop, one of the last of his race. Wolfgang returned, in the autumn of the same year, to Italy; and, not long after, back again to Salzburg.

It is usual to take account of the work done during the lives even of the greatest men, when they are ended. In Mozart's case it becomes convenient, and indeed necessary, to reckon up the achievements of his boyhood. At the age of sixteen he was the finest *Clavecinist* in the world. He had produced two "Requiems," a "Stabat Mater," various Offertories, Hymns, and Motets, two Cantatas, four Operas, thirteen Symphonies, twenty-four pianoforte Sonatas, besides many Quartets, Trios, and Concertos for individual instruments, military Divertimentos, Marches, &c. &c. All this the work of a youth, half of whose life had been spent in travelling and public exhibition!

But neither Mozart's prodigious talents nor reputation produced the slightest effect on his immediate fortunes. The aim and object in life of every German artist, great or small, of the last century, seems to have been *a place*. Mozart presented no exception to this rule; for his earnings, like those of most of his contempories, were not only small but precarious. The Prince-Bishop of Salzburg would have nothing to say to him.

The Elector of Bavaria found him too young. The Elector Palatine had nothing fit for him vacant. He visited Paris again, in the hopes of getting an opera-book to set, but without success. At length he returned once more to his old quarters at Salzburg, where (in 1779) he was made Organist of the Court, and soon after of the Cathedral.

The following year is an epoch in his life, and in the history of modern music. In 1780 the composition of a grand opera, "Idomeneo," was confided to him by the new Elector of Bavaria, Charles Theodore. It was produced at Munich, in January, 1781, with a success altogether extraordinary, considering the dulness of the libretto and—the originality of the music; for, works of art may be too much in advance, as well as in arrear, of public taste. The judgment of no audience was ever more severely tested than of that which assisted at the first representation of "Idomeneo." No such a step in advance of all preceding music of the same kind had ever been taken before. Construction, detail, instrumentation—everything in it was unprecedented. It was a work in which the best qualities of the music of all nations, and of all ages, were found aggregated and made homogeneous. The painter Tintoret wrote over the door of his studio "the drawing of Michael Angelo and the colouring of Titian." Mozart might have written on the score of his "Idomeneo," "the majesty of Palestrina, the sweetness of Pergolesi, the science of Bach, the clearness of Handel, and more things of my own than were ever dreamt of, even in the philosophy of these great men."

I must ask your leave still farther to prolong this already prolonged session by introducing to you a passage, suggested by this first performance, from one of the most delightful and now one of the scarcest of books about music, Oulibicheff's "Nouvelle Biographie de Mozart."*

The elder Mozart did not wait for an account of the first per

* Moscow, 1843. Vol. ii. 142.

formance of "Idomeneo" to be brought to him. To have denied himself the pleasure of hearing the work itself would have been to have denied himself some of the recompense of his twenty years of devotion and self-denial. Accompanied by his daughter, he reached Munich on the 26th of January, the eve of his son's birthday and of the production of his opera . . . The success was complete. The audience was enthusiastic, and demonstrated its enthusiasm unrestrainedly with voice, hand, and foot. But who will venture to describe the condition of the old man who, ensconced in a corner of the orchestra, might have been observed, doubtful of the evidence even of his own well-trained ears, as they conveyed to his inner sense, one after another, the melody, the harmony, and the orchestration of "Idomeneo." Let us figure to ourselves a man at upwards of sixty years of age finding the greatest pleasure he had ever known; a learned and appreciative musician in the ecstasy only to be created by music of which neither he nor any one else had ever formed even an approximate conception. Mozart's master assisting at the first universal lesson given by his pupil to the world; the pupil whose little fingers he had guided on the key-board while they were as yet too feeble to express on paper the ideas which a brain of only five years had been able to conceive; that pupil whom God himself had confided to his charge; the end of his existence, his glory, his happiness, his all, his only son. Then and there the task of the old man was done; then and there came to an end the relations of authority and dependence between father and son which "Idomeneo" rather than manhood had in a moment brought to an end. We take leave here of Leopold Mozart, the wise, the good, the self-denying; who with admirable perseverance, sagacity and devotion, had consecrated the faculties with which Heaven had endowed him to the cultivation of faculties greater than his own. So the lapidary reduces to powder the common diamonds that lie about him, to cut and polish the single jewel, priceless and unequalled, with which he is about to decorate an imperial crown.

From this time the greatness of Mozart's genius was admitted by all the world—even by the Prince-Bishop of Salzburg. I have but time to give the dates of some of his greatest subsequent productions.

"Il Seraglio" followed soon on "Idomeneo." The "Six Quartets" dedicated to Haydn appeared in 1785. In 1786 he wrote and produced "Le Nozze di Figaro," and in the following year, "Don Giovanni." To 1788 we owe "Così fan Tutte," and to '91 (his last year), "Die Zauberflöte" and the stupendous "Requiem," the crowning glory of his marvellous career.

In the intervals of these large and exquisitely finished productions he extemporized rather than composed the majority of those great symphonies without one or more of which no series of orchestral concerts ever passes over; the majority of those masses, hardly less familiar even in Protestant England, than the most favourite oratorios of Handel; the majority of those quintets and quartets for stringed instruments which are household words with every *virtuoso* great or small; concertos and sonatas innumerable for the piano; pieces for all instruments, and all combinations of instruments; single offertorios, motets, songs, duets—it is useless continuing the list. If we add to all this that Mozart was, from infancy a public performer, and from early manhood a musical director and a not inactive teacher, we must admit that in thirty-five years he did the work of a long life. The least acquainted with the results of this work will know how complete, how finished they are. It can hardly be said that he spared no pains, for he did all things as easily as he did them well.

I shall not trouble you with any formal summing-up or presentation of my own opinions as to the place Mozart holds among composers. One musician—I hesitate to put even the possibility of this before you—one musician, a successor, may nave exhibited greater genius; he now and then perhaps has surpassed Mozart; his means were greater, for he began life when Mozart ended it. One other, a predecessor, may have excelled Mozart in learning; he had time to do so, for he lived to the age of sixty-five. But surely no composer has combined genius and learning in such perfect proportions, none has been able to dignify the lightest and the tritest forms by such profound scholarship, or, at the moment when he was drawing most largely on the resources of musical science, to appear so natural, so spontaneous, and so thoroughly at ease

THE FOURTH PERIOD

(Continued).

EXTINCTION OF ALL TRACES OF OLD TONALITY IN THE WORKS OF MOZART—BEETHOVEN—HIS THREE "MANNERS"—HIS ORATORIO, FIRST MASS AND OPERA—BEETHOVEN AS A CONTRAPUNTIST—THE ORCHESTRAL SYMPHONY—ITS DIFFICULTIES—BEETHOVEN'S THIRD "MANNER"—HIS LOSS OF HEARING—SPOHR—MENDELSSOHN—SCHUBERT—SCHUMANN—STERNDALE BENNETT.

THE FOURTH PERIOD

(*Continued*).

My division of musical history into periods has been dictated, not by the accidental and external forms of the music written during the centuries, half-centuries, decades or even single years of which I have had to speak, but by the internal structure of this music, and the principles on which it is certain its composers worked. The musicians of the Second Period (it has been my principal object in this course to bring this out) took a wholly different view of the nature of the scale from those of the Fourth; and the inevitable results of this were melody, harmony, and a mode of developing musical thoughts essentially unlike.

Traces of this old "tonality" or theory of the scale, may be found in the works of almost every composer, of whatever nation, down to about the middle of the last century; in those of the first generation of the Neapolitan School, and of their contemporaries in other parts of Italy, in Germany, France, and England. It is possible even that some of these—echoes of echoes of voices themselves long silent—might be visible to a keen eye, or audible to a delicate ear, in the earlier works of Haydn. In those of his manhood and later life there are none whatever. Many of Haydn's musical expressions (I say it with all possible reverence) have become old-fashioned; but I do not know one which could with propriety be called ancient. Haydn therefore is justly regarded as the founder, or father, of modern music. Original and elegant as were the compositions of his predecessor, C. P. Emmanuel Bach, to whom both he and Mozart avowedly owed so much, the influence of his great father and teacher, J. Sebastian Bach, is continually discernible in them; and though the modern sonata, quartet, and symphony are there clearly enough foreshadowed, that *form*, which is now the inalienable characteristic, nay even the condition of existence, of such pieces, was never fully developed in them.

The works of Mozart are essentially modern, in plan as in detail; those of the last ten years of his life may be regarded as types of the Fourth Period. In them he is never even old-fashioned. He uses now and then an "old and antique" figure, but always consciously and always finely. Barring these occasional tributes of respect to the memory of the sixteenth century, he is, in melody, harmony, treatment, and instrumentation, modern in thought, note, and deed.

Mozart died before he had attained his thirty-sixth year—prematurely, if life be measured by time only; but surely not so, if it be measured by labour. Nevertheless it is difficult to resist speculating on the future which might have been but was never to be his; and impossible not to feel regret that at least a few more years had not been accorded to one so able and so eager to turn them to account. But the additional steps which we picture him to ourselves as making in these possible years would probably have proved beyond the strength of one who had already travelled so far. The efforts of no single man, whether crowded into the shortest or spread over the longest life, could have been equal to the exploration or exhaustion of the enormous world of thought which Mozart's genius had opened up. The work however has not been unattempted, nor unachieved—though by another hand. A few days after Mozart's death Beethoven entered his twenty-first year.

Ludwig van Beethoven was born, in 1770, at Bonn, on the Rhine. His father, a tenor singer in the service of the Elector of Cologne, taught him the elements of music, for which, very unlike Mozart, he is said to have shown, in his boyhood, but little inclination. Subsequently however after having received some lessons from Vander Eden, Organist of the Court, he began to exhibit both liking and aptitude for the art. On the death of Vander Eden, being then twelve years of age, he became the pupil of his successor, Neefe,—an excellent musician, and a man whose discernment was justified in the subsequent career of Beethoven, of whose already remarkable faculty he became early cognizant. Another and a greater, at a later epoch, appreciated his power, and even foretold his future eminence. In the year 1790, Beethoven, being then twenty, extemporized on the pianoforte in the presence of Mozart, who for some time listened to him with indifference, thinking that his so-called "extemporization" had been prepared and that he was playing from memory. Mortified at this indifference, and still more at the cause of it, Beethoven insisted on Mozart himself giving him a subject. This, though chosen for the purpose of testing his powers to the utmost, he treated with such skill and felicity, that Mozart rose from his seat, and walking on tiptoe and holding his breath, for fear of troubling the rich stream of music which was winding about him, passed into another room where some friends were seated, and said, "Listen to this young man; you'll hear him talked about some of these days."

Shortly after this (in 1793) he left Bonn for Vienna, in order to put himself under the instruction of Haydn, who, it is said, at once appreciated his genius, and understood with what sort of pupil he should have to deal. Haydn was however at that time in the act of preparation for his second visit to London, and he handed over Beethoven to the care of his friend Albrechtsberger, a musician whose learning was in inverse ratio to his invention, and who might therefore have been thought likely to prove a much better teacher than Haydn himself. There is however such a thing as a genius for teaching, as well as for composing; and with this Albrechtsberger seems to have been but poorly endowed. A good master for a docile, easy-going pupil, he found himself altogether unable to deal with a young man of genius and very strong will, entering life in the fourth year of the French Revolution, and very decidedly averse to taking anything for granted.

Beethoven, whose mechanical skill as well as inventive faculty were much in advance of his science, soon drew attention on himself by his extempore pianoforte playing which, by all accounts, was at this time truly marvellous. In this kind of performance a certain amount of preparation theoretical and practical being assumed, audacity is, like action to the orator, the first, second, and third requisite. The *Improvisatore* who hesitates is lost. He may fail in this or that, but before all things he must dare. In self-reliance Beethoven was, from youth to age, the strongest of human creatures; and with reason. For, into the nature of those forces through which he was destined to move the affections of men, he saw deeper than it had ever been given before to man to see ; and he knew it. Yet in this most resolute and gifted youth was there no deficiency of that good sense which, however often it may be dissociated from mere fancy, is a necessary complement of imagination. At the very moment that Beethoven was astounding his Viennese audiences by the originality, and perhaps very often the strangeness and even uncouthness of his extemporaneous inspirations, his compositions, destined to remain in written notes, to be tested by readers and hearers unwarmed by the personal influence of their author, were as regularly planned as the dullest exercise that ever came out of the best-regulated conservatory in Europe. It is true that certain pieces, composed in his boyhood, of which this would not be true, had found their way, through the indiscreet zeal of friends, into print; but these Beethoven always repudiated and ignored, never allowing them even to be mentioned in his presence. In his acknowledged first works the influence of Mozart may be clearly traced; not in a parrot-like imitation of mere manner, but in the sentiment of which that manner is but the expression, and in the adoption of that form of composition which, though not the invention of Mozart, nor even of Haydn, was first perfectly carried out in the works of those great masters.

The events of Beethoven's external life are few, and of course altogether inferior in interest to the story, only to be read in his works, of the development of his genius. The tremendous conflicts and the prodigious changes of which the French Revolution was the immediate cause, threw the whole artist race on their own resources, during the last years of the last century. The innumerable "places" which had afforded at least bread and peace, on conditions however humiliating, more especially to the musicians of Germany, fell one after another with the small Principalities, to many of which they had long furnished the best excuse for existence. The death of the Elector of Cologne, who had been a kind and judicious patron to Beethoven, anticipated in his case the loss of help to which political causes would a little later have inevitably subjected him. At this time (1801) he was thirty-one years of age; and though the eyes and ears of the judicious few had been long watchful of his progress, his reputation, from a variety of causes, personal perhaps no less than political, was in no degree so extended as that of most of his great predecessors, at the same age. His existence was ignored at the Imperial Court, and his Public, however "judicious," remained comparatively small. In 1809 he had determined to accept the office of Chapel-master to the then King of Westphalia, Jerome Bonaparte, when the Archduke Rodolph and two other noble amateurs resolved to save him to Austria by insuring him a means of living. Deeply moved by this tribute to his genius, he abandoned his project of emigration and remained, for life as it proved, at Vienna. Beethoven died in the year 1827, at the age of fifty-seven.

The biographers of Beethoven have generally agreed to divide his life into three "periods," and his works into three corresponding "manners." The first period extends from 1795, the year of his first acknowledged publication, to 1804; the second from 1804 to 1814; and the third from 1814 to 1827, the year of his death.

To the *second* of these periods belong the majority of the works of Beethoven which have attained the greatest favour, as yet; his one Oratorio, "The Mount of Olives;" his one Opera, "Fidelio;" the first of his two Masses, that in C; most of his single songs, *e.g.* "Ah! Perfido," and "Adelaida;" the Choral Fantasia, the Overture and other music to Goethe's "Egmont." Some of his best pieces of instrumental chamber-music, among them the majority of his Sonatas for the pianoforte, were products of these ten years; and to these must be added the still more precious results of a still higher aim. Beethoven is the composer of nine Orchestral Symphonies, every one richer in detail and larger in outline than the one before it. Of these no less than six, all but the first two and the last, belong to this second period.

On Beethoven's only attempt at Oratorio, the best criticism that can be made is that it is the only attempt. Of what may be not improperly styled the epic in music, Beethoven is the greatest master the world has yet seen. In the dramatic also he exhibited a faculty which, exercised more frequently, would without doubt have attained to something like the same perfection and pre-eminence. But to that mixture of the dramatic and the epic which is needed for the oratorio of modern times, Beethoven, from whatever cause, failed in giving the proper proportions. There is no reticence about the "Mount of Olives:" everything in it is made out, nothing suggested or implied; and we shudder to find persons and events, never to be contemplated without awe or mentioned above breath, thrust into the full blaze of day, and subjected to the same treatment as human actors, their feelings and concerns. There is no reason why the "Mount of Olives" should not serve for the next miracle play at Ammergau. Who would think of turning Handel's "Messiah" or Mendelssohn's "Elijah" to such an account? There is reason to believe that Beethoven planned, but he certainly never executed, another oratorio.

Nor can the Mass in C, abounding as it does in beautiful detail, be regarded as a work in its class of the highest order. The Christian world, whose taste, formed on models which, though varying from age to age in external form, have all an internal structure highly artificial and exquisitely elaborate, is not yet prepared for an altogether new style of Church music. This indeed Beethoven did not attempt; and his training had not prepared him to work in the old and accepted style. The Church music of Haydn and Mozart is often open to the charge of secularity; but the charge is no sooner made than it has to be abandoned. The learning, more especially of the latter master, makes itself felt at every instant; and some profound musical artifice soon redeems the momentary lapse into which a too gay humour or, it may have been, carelessness had betrayed him. Beethoven never appears to so little advantage as when, or I would rather say, never appears to any disadvantage save when, he attempts contrapuntal artifice. In this he had no sufficient training as a youth, and it was not likely, perhaps not possible, that he should undergo it as a man. Contrapuntal skill is equally wanting to the first Mass, composed in 1807, and to the second, finished in 1822. Compare the fugue in the former, so pompously begun and so soon abandoned, on the words "Cum Sancto Spiritu," with any of the many similar movements in the masses of Haydn or Mozart. Perhaps it will be replied that this was, on Beethoven's part, a matter of choice,

N

not of necessity; that he worked in and for the nineteenth century; that the child of the French Revolution had no concern with the effete forms of the *Ancien Régime.* Not so. Beethoven has more than once measured himself as a contrapuntist with the greatest of his predecessors. Turn to the instrumental prelude to the last movement of the Mass in D, one of his latest works; here surely he has avowedly "rushed on" to the track trodden by Mozart in the "Recordare" of his "Requiem." Compare the two. See how in Mozart the themes appear and reappear, subject to every kind of inversion; observe the sparse yet sufficient modulation, the boldness of the combinations, in which transitory harshness relieves average suavity. Turn then to Beethoven; study his too evident attempt to do something of the same kind. Dwell for a moment, if your ear can bear it, on some of the combinations; listen to the vain repetitions; follow out the restless modulation;—you will then understand the difference between the "ripe scholar" whose training betrays itself in the slightest expression, and the incomplete practitioner, whose every attempt at seeming learned is too apt to result in being clumsy and unmeaning.

Happily however these attempts, on the part of Beethoven, were few and far between. If he knew his strength, he knew his weakness: possibly indeed caring too little about it to try to overcome it, and content, as well he might be, to do what he did best, better than it had ever been done before.

If the estimation in which a work of art should be held has any relation to the difficulty of producing it, and to its consequent rarity, then assuredly the Orchestral Symphony must be regarded as holding, beyond all comparison, the first place among musical works. Of the composers of the Fourth Period whose names are in the Chronological Tables,* the majority have not even attempted this form of composition, and the

* See the end of this volume.

number of those who have succeeded indisputably in it may be told on the fingers:—it amounts to five, or at the utmost, to seven. Even of those who have done so in the analogous form of the Overture, many have failed in, or have judiciously abstained from attempting, the more sustained labour of the Symphony. Nor, again, is success in Opera any guarantee for the satisfactory exercise of that unaided strength which a well-developed series of instrumental movements demands. In opera, even in oratorio, the composer is helped at every step by the incidents with which he has to deal, and by the sentiment, and even the changing metre, of the words he has to set. Add to this the fact that, in addition to all the means of expression which are at the command of the symphony writer—artificial pipes and strings in any number—the opera composer has at his one more powerful still than any of these—the human voice. The composition of an instrumental Quartet might seem a still greater achievement than that of a Symphony; seeing that the means and appliances of the composer are even fewer. But the same development, though in some instances attained, is not looked for in the former as in the latter. The quartet too affords no scope for the exercise of one of the most difficult parts of a composer's art, the successive presentation to the best advantage, and the blending into a perfect whole, of the instruments, so many and so various in their quality and force, which form the modern orchestra.

No work of art is so thoroughly abstract, so completely cut off from the support of extraneous interest, as an orchestral symphony. Half our interest in a building grows out of our knowledge of its purposes and use; half the charm of a picture or a statue is due to its resemblance to some existing natural type. But a piece of instrumental music serves no obvious purpose, has no obvious use; nor can it, save imperfectly or ridiculously, imitate anything. It addresses itself to the ear, but the impression it makes may vary infinitely with the humour of him who receives it. The instant it attempts to be practical—to present definitely this or that scene, or to make out this or that sentiment—it becomes another and an inferior thing. Of the first eight symphonies of Beethoven the favourite, among persons of small musical culture, is that known as the "Pastoral." And the very things in it which give them the most pleasure are just those which the cultured hearer would most like to strike out of it. He will follow the composer, in his saunter along the brookside, with complacency and something more, so long as what he hears suggests to him the same frame of mind as the brookside has suggested to the composer; but the instant the cuckoo and the nightingale appear upon the scene, and suggestion gives place to imitation, as in this Pastoral Symphony, he feels that Art has overstepped its limits. The figures on the canvas swell into relief; the cheeks of the statue glow under the action of the rouge-pot. We know not what may be coming next; and we prick up our ears for the bark of the cur, the bray of the jackass, or any other of the cacophonies of the field and the farmyard. "Sonate," said a witty eighteenth-century Frenchman, with no music in his soul, "Sonate, que veux-tu?—What do you mean?—what do you want?—what have you to say to me?" The answer would inevitably be as useless as is the question; for Wits and Sonatas speak different languages, and are ignorant of one another's. Do not inquire too curiously what this or that passage of music, pure and simple, means. Be assured it has a meaning; and a meaning which we shall get at through our sensibilities, not our intelligences.

Now, of this form of art—for a symphony is but a sonata lengthened and widened, not always deepened—of this most difficult form of art, Beethoven is beyond question the greatest master that has yet appeared. In it he has exceeded his predecessors; and what is more extraordinary still, he remains unequalled, perhaps unapproached, by any of his successors. One overture, "Die Zauberflöte," and one movement, the last of the Symphony in C of Mozart (the Jupiter), remain unrivalled monuments of the eclectic in music. In them is combined with the contrapuntal science of the Second and Third Periods, the passion, energy, power of expression and form of the Fourth. This combination Beethoven rarely attempted and never succeeded in making. Like all great geniuses, he worked out his own purposes in his own way.

Not to waste time on mere eulogy, it may be said that Beethoven's symphonies exhibit an enlarged, and as they get later a continually enlarging, plan, in comparison with those of any foregoing master. The richness of his invention in detail is inexhaustible, yet never drawn upon to excess. His manner of working illustrates this very happily. He is said to have spent hours, days, weeks, or it might be months, in the elaboration of his scores; but his process of elaboration was the reverse of that of most artists. It consisted, not in putting in, but in cutting out, effects often beautiful in themselves, but which he thought, or knew, would come into mischievous contact with others. To this is due, no doubt, to some extent, the grand simplicity, the breadth of the majority of his creations. If Beethoven is ever obscure (I speak now of the works of his second period), it is because his thought is hard to penetrate. All that lucid exposition can do to make it intelligible he does. The plan of his works exhibits an original peculiarity; the introduction of episodes, in the course of which thoughts which in the main are principal, become subordinate. The practice he sometimes adopts of linking his movements together, passing almost insensibly from the one to the other, was, though uncommon when he adopted it, not original. The earliest instance of it with which I am acquainted, is in one of the works of C. P. Emmanuel Bach, who introduces the slow movement of his Sonata in A,* by a modulation at the end of the movement

* See Fétis's "Œuvres Choisies de E. Bach," pp. 57-8. Paris: Schönenberger.

immediately preceding. The works of Beethoven present many examples of startling harmonic progression; so many indeed that, in inferior hands they would soon cease to startle and still sooner to please. But his variety in these, as in everything else, is inexhaustible. Even when one of his figures reappears in another part of the same movement, the effect of it, from its new position or some fresh arrangement of its component parts, has all the charm of perfect novelty. Perhaps, more than in any other individual peculiarity, Beethoven is most decidedly original in his rhythm. No conceivable length of phrase, no variety in the distribution of the notes of it, seems unmanageable or uncouth, with him. In his works this resource has become almost a new art, of which he is at once the inventor, and so far the greatest master.

Nothing that could be said in praise of the majority of the works composed by Beethoven before the year 1814, or thereabouts, especially of his symphonies, would be likely to meet with dissent at the present day. The originality of his conceptions, and still more, I am certain, the mechanical difficulties of realizing them in performance, presented formidable barriers to their full appreciation, even by a very recent generation of musicians. Musical knowledge and musical skill have however become so much commoner and greater among the present generation, especially of English artists, that many a performance which would have been a rare *Solennité* five-and-twenty years since, is now a thing of everyday occurrence. Opportunities for studying these works through the ear are now neither few nor far to seek.

But, in respect to the later productions of Beethoven, opinions are by no means so accordant. On the one hand, it is held that the great poet of sound went "from strength to strength," always at an increasing ratio; and that the true measure of the excellence of his works is to the last their chronology. On the other hand, it is said that this rule only holds good up to a certain point of time; and that those of his so-called third period, though of course presenting more or less matter for admiration, are extravagant or altogether wanting in design, very deficient in melody, and disfigured by absurd and even hideous effects.

This extraordinary and indeed altogether exceptional termination to the career of a great musician is accounted for, by those who assume it, in the growing influence of that awful visitation which overshadowed so large a portion of the life of Beethoven; his loss of hearing, with all its possible consequences, unusually aggravated with him—isolation, distrust, and eventually misanthropy. But this visitation, alas! was not exclusively reserved for the last years of this 'most unhappy man of men;' the consciousness of it dawned upon him before he had reached his thirtieth year, as early indeed as 1796; and the calamity, in its full proportions, made its horrible presence felt only four years later—*i.e.*, before the commencement even of that second period during which what are commonly thought to be his best works were written. That the farther years removed the deaf musician from concrete music, the more difficult he would find it to realize his own conceptions, is possible, if not certain; but that any space of time could have power altogether to incapacitate so great a genius from hearing with his mind's ear better than ordinary men with their body's, it is impossible to believe. Increasing gloom and growing irritability might deepen the sadness of his conceptions, and occasionally contort the forms in which he sought to express them; but I cannot see why the conceptions themselves should ever cease to be noble, or the forms intelligible, to those who have patience and humility to make them out.

With some of the later works of Beethoven I cannot pretend to an intimate acquaintance; but there are others, among them the great work of his last years, the Ninth or "Choral" Symphony, which I have had occasion to study with profound attention. If the remaining works of Beethoven's third period have any analogy with this (which for the present I must take leave to assume they have), I would say to those who do not understand and, therefore, do not like them; study them, look at them, and listen to them till you do.

I will not apologize for occupying so much of our last hour together in the contemplation of this gigantic figure, which assuredly "doth bestride" not merely my lecture, but the first half of the nineteenth century, "like a Colossus." It is time, however, for me to pass on to his all but contemporary, Spohr, whose lot it was to survive him by more than thirty years; to Mendelssohn, so much the junior of both; and to those very few who have worked at all successfully in the same high class of composition.

The life of Louis Spohr has been given to the world in an autobiography,* very recently published, which I heartily commend to your notice and perusal. Musical literature is so poor in this class that, even if from this cause only, Spohr's account of himself should be read. It is, however, worth reading for its own sake. Spohr's career was not deficient in adventure; he travelled much, and heard music wherever music at all special was to be heard. But the book is, I think, chiefly remarkable as a study of self-contemplation, and as a revelation of self-contentment, without parallel in literature; except, perhaps, in the autobiography of an artist very unlike Spohr in every other respect, Benvenuto Cellini.

Spohr, who was born in 1784, when Beethoven was fourteen years of age, and who died as recently as 1860, aged seventy-six, was undoubtedly a man of genius, and a great musician; but if, as is not impossible, posterity should come to the conclusion that his works are, on the whole, the least great which have come from the pens of the greatest composers of the Fourth Period, the result will inevitably be attributable to his having adopted a *genus* in music, the "chromatic," which, how-

* An English translation of it has since appeared.

ever valuable as a decoration and a resource, can never serve for the substance of that which is to stand the wear and tear of everyday use.

His music holds the same relation to that of Mozart and Haydn that Flamboyant Gothic does to the Second Pointed style. The traditions of a good and beautiful thing are in it, but with its accidents exaggerated, and its essentials weakened. What Mozart and Haydn, and even Handel and Bach, do sometimes, Spohr does always. His manifest dread of harshness has seriously impaired the vigour, and his fondness for intricate construction the clearness, of his music. No great composer seems to repeat himself so often; for the simple reason that his principal means are just those which other great composers use only as subordinate. However various may be his designs, he has but one manner of carrying them out. Strangely enough too Spohr carries his manner into every kind of composition; for he has essayed every kind. Be his subject grave or gay, lively or severe, he never, if he can help it, leaves a tone undivided, never uses an essential note when he can put an altered one in its place.

The favour with which even the earliest compositions of Felix Mendelssohn were received, and the great and increasing estimation in which they are held, are due mainly of course to their intrinsic excellence, but incidentally to the contrast which they present to the works of Spohr who, for any influence he exercised on his younger contemporary, might never have existed. In the works of Mendelssohn traces enough may be found of his familiarity with Beethoven, with Mozart, and, more than all perhaps, with J. Sebastian Bach, of whose spirit he has caught much, and of whom he is, in a certain sense, the representative in this Fourth Period; of Spohr there are none whatever.

Mendelssohn was the most learned musician of genius that had appeared since the death of Mozart, with whom, indeed, he presents so many points of resemblance, in his outer as well as his inner life, that no reader of musical history can fail to be struck by them. Like Mozart's, Mendelssohn's career began, and alas! ended, early; he barely passed the middle of the way of our life, and was lost to the world at the moment when his ripened genius and fascinating character made him most precious to those who were at all familiar with his works or his person. In the fecundity of his invention he was certainly inferior to his antitype; but more propitious times and circumstances enabled him to exercise it at his will, and put within his reach the greatest privilege of life, the power of choosing his work. Happily his inclinations and his aspirations, like his powers, were of the noblest order. Mendelssohn's compositions, always of high excellence, are also in the highest class of excellence. The symphony, the concert overture, the cantata, and more especially the oratorio, by turns claimed the exercise of his noble imagination or elegant fancy, of his pure taste and profound scholarship. In one style only, the dramatic, his power was unproved—though not altogether untried.

I said just now that the number of composers who have succeeded indisputably in the symphony is five, or at the utmost seven. The two whom many, perhaps all German, musical students would add to it are Schubert and Schumann.

I must restrict myself to very narrow limits in respect to the outer lives of these two composers, about whom much has within the last few years been written which is easily accessible.

Franz Schubert was born at Vienna in 1797. His musical education was begun early, and among his first instructors was Salieri, once regarded as a formidable rival of Mozart! Schubert had the good fortune to belong to a family passionately given to the study and practice of music, in association with whom he became betimes familiar with the best chamber music of the best masters. The greater part of his short life was spent in

Vienna, in unaccountable obscurity; and it is only since his death, in 1828, at the age of thirty-one, that his reputation, even as a song-writer, has been at all commensurate with his merits; and only within comparatively few years that even the existence of his more extended works has become known.

Robert Schumann was born at Zwickau in Saxony, in 1810. Though, like Schubert, he began music early, he exhibited neither liking nor talent for it till his ninth year, when the one was awakened, and the other brought to light by the performance of the great pianist and musician, Moscheles, then entering on the splendid career only recently brought to a close. The impetus thus received was not however maintained by judicious discipline, and Schumann's attention if not his affection, was whiled away from music by the charms of her sister, poetry. He became an ardent devotee of the school of which Jean Paul in Germany and Byron in England were the most prominent representatives. After passing some time as a student, nominally at least, of Law, at the Universities of Leipzig and Heidelberg, he determined, at the age of twenty, to devote himself entirely to the art which he had never ceased to love and, though immethodically, to cultivate, and was received among the pupils of Friedrick Wieck, one of the most eminent and successful pianoforte teachers of his time, whose daughter and pupil, the illustrious Clara Schumann, he subsequently married. A foolish attempt to accelerate his progress as a pianist by an unnatural treatment of one of his fingers brought his progress as an executant to a premature close; a circumstance the less to be regretted as it threw him seriously, for the first time, on the study and practice of composition and orchestration. These he varied by the exercise of his pen in criticism, an exercise for which his general culture singularly qualified him. It is sad to have to record that Schumann's last years were darkened by the most grievous, because the most hopeless, of afflictions. From this he was relieved in 1857, at the early age of forty-seven.

Of these two composers the former must, I think, be regarded as the more inventive, the latter as the more skilful. The isolated songs of Schubert, from their beauty, fitness, freshness and number, place him in general estimation, and deservedly, at the head of all song-writers, of whatever age or country. As a practitioner on a more extended scale, a composer of symphonies, and of chamber music symphonic in its scope and character, his place is lower. He is rich in, nay replete with, ideas of which he is rather the slave than the master. His "form" is often, and is obviously generally meant to be, that of his great predecessors and contemporaries; and his principal themes are always worthy of their position. But subordinate figures crowd into his work in such force and number as often to obliterate the one and disturb the proportions of the other. True, these same subordinate figures are many of them unspeakably beautiful; but like ones in equal numbers must have prayed for admission to the works of other artists who, better disciplined, have had the self-denial to keep them out. As a consequence, Schubert never seems to have known when his work was done. He is diffuse to an extent far beyond the practice of any other composer of like power. There is music enough in any one of his symphonies to set up a musician, of inferior invention but superior skill, with two or three better ones. If ever Schubert's reputation as a symphony writer dies, it will be of the plethora of invention exhibited in them.

In these respects Schumann presents the most complete contrast to Schubert that any so considerable an artist could do to another often regarded as his equal. His extended movements are admirably planned, sufficiently and not too richly decorated with subordinate ideas; and they leave on the mind a sense of proportion which is of itself a source of pleasure. His power of pursuing a musical idea to its utmost consequences—and never beyond them—is on a par with that of the greatest masters. But it cannot be said that the idea is always worth the pursuit.

He is tuneful; but his tune is often queer, odd, *bizarre;* seldom graceful, hardly ever seemingly spontaneous.

To the names of these seven masters of the symphonic style, all long silent, I must now, alas! add another, that of a compatriot quite recently taken from us, William Sterndale Bennett. Whether a national style of instrumental music is a possibility is a question. Instrumental music doubtless owes its origin to the dance; and so long as it retained traces of this origin its nationality might still have been discernible. Little by little, however, these traces have faded; and music pure and simple, music unconnected with the acted or unacted drama, has assumed more and more decidedly the character of a universal language. It would be difficult or impossible, were the nationality of Bennett unknown, to pronounce upon it from the unsupported evidence of his music. That it should present indications of German influence was inevitable. In the works of German masters alone could the principles of the symphonic school be found exemplified, and Bennett profited by them, as did Milton by those of his predecessors of Greece and Italy, or Pope by those of his French contemporaries. But there is enough and more than enough in the works of Bennett to distinguish them from those of any of his predecessors or contemporaries of whatever nationality, among the greatest of whom he is assuredly entitled to a place,—what place time, which has hardly yet determined that of his friend Mendelssohn can alone determine.

THE FOURTH PERIOD

(Continued).

THE LYRIC DRAMA—THE "LIBRETTO"—ITALIAN OPERA—PICCINNI — PAER — ROSSINI — DONIZETTI — BELLINI — GERMAN OPERA—WEBER—FRENCH OPERA—LULLY—RAMEAU—"LES ITALIENS"—GLUCK AND PICCINNI—CHERUBINI—SPONTINI—ROSSINI—HALÉVY—AUBER—THE MUSIC "OF THE FUTURE."

THE FOURTH PERIOD

(Continued).

Of the great masters of the Symphonic School, nine in all, with whom my last lecture was exclusively occupied, only one, Mozart, can be said to have succeeded in the Lyric Drama; and the instances in which even he has done so perfectly must be reduced to two, perhaps even to one, "Don Giovanni;" so many conditions, over and above and beside musical genius and culture, must be fulfilled to make a successful opera; not the least of these being that most despised and most rare literary product, a good libretto. The absence of this no amount of genius, science, or tact in a composer has ever been found able to supply. A thousand failures could be brought in evidence of this truth, which however is better and more easily proved by one fact; that the history of Opera centres itself, neither in Italy, nor in Germany,—but in France. Not that the best or most popular operas of modern times are all the works of Frenchmen, though some of them assuredly are, but that of those which are the works even of Italians or Germans the majority have been set to French librettos, and produced on the French stage. Of the last century of Italian opera one single composer survives, Cimarosa; and he in one single work, "Il Matrimonio Segreto." This survival of a single production, out of eighty by the same master, would be unaccountable did we not know that the music is happily married, possibly to very mortal verse, but to verse which is made to unfold interesting events in an orderly and intelligible manner. I believe "Il Matrimonio Segreto" was adapted directly from our Colman and Garrick's "Clandestine Marriage." Its Italian costume sits as easily upon it as though it had never worn another. Perhaps, after all, its bib and tucker were Italian. Let me, in passing, direct your attention to the fact that this opera, generally regarded and spoken of as an antiquated work, was composed and produced in Vienna in the year 1793—two years after the death of Mozart. Cimarosa died (ætat. 47) in 1801.

But of Cimarosa's immediate predecessors, Guglielmi, Sacchini, Salieri; of his contemporaries, Paisiello, Zingarelli, Sarti, who, in the present generation, knows anything? Fragments from the structures they raised, to contemporary eyes so substantial and enduring, are exhumed from time to time, for the gratification of the curious; but the Elgin marbles are as little likely to look down again on the worship of Minerva, as these fragments to be restored to their places, within the walls of any existing theatre.

Let us see what has been done on the lyric stage of these three peoples, the Italian, the German, and the French, since we last quitted it.

Italian opera in the Fourth Period begins with Piccinni, of whom I shall have to speak presently in his connexion with the French stage. I will only note for the moment that in his opera "La buona Figliuola" is to be found the first example and subsequent type of the modern Finale of more than one movement. Of his contemporaries and immediate successors, those at least who attained the greatest success, I have already mentioned some of the most distinguished, as being utterly forgotten. Of the numerous and generally successful operas of Fernando Paer (an Italian, his name notwithstanding) one, "Agnese," lives in the recollection of aged amateurs through the transcendent presentation of the principal character by the eminent singer and actor Ambrogetti. Another, "I Fuorusciti," may also be remembered through an English adaptation given in London not many years ago. For the rest, they and their author, whose "Laodicea" was not brought to an end, on the night of its first production, because of the numerous encores, live only in the speech made to the latter by Beethoven, in relation to one of them, "Fidelio." "I like your opera very much, and I mean to set it to music," said the truculent master; which he did, as we all know. Italian opera still lives, but lives only through four composers, Rossini, Donizetti, Bellini, and Verdi.

The early works of Rossini, born at Pesaro in 1792, notwithstanding their enticing tunefulness, the variety and strength of their orchestration and a vivacity too enjoyable in itself to allow the hearer to question its fitness for the situation, have already, in many instances been relegated to the limbo of forgotten things. Of upwards of forty, the first bearing date 1810, the last 1829, how few have kept the stage! "Il Barbiere" (1816), "Otello" (1816), "La Gazza Ladra" (1817), and "Semiramide" (1823), are the only ones, I think, that can fairly be called current. And the permanent success of the first in this short list is not altogether due to the music, fresh and captivating as it still is. The libretto is based on a French comedy, the scheme and development of which rank it among the masterpieces of dramatic construction. Admirable and admired as these and perhaps others of his works unquestionably are, Europe is gradually accepting the decision of Paris, and accustoming itself to look upon Rossini as "The composer of Guillaume Tell;" and this notwithstanding the amazing want of interest, and the loose construction of the poet's share in that great work. Strange that the most skilful theatrical artificers in Europe should have found nothing better than this inane production for the greatest composer they have ever sought to naturalize to employ his talents upon. More strange, if true, that the composer himself should have chosen this libretto, out of several offered to him; among them Scribe's "La Juive," afterwards set by Halévy; a drama so interesting and so well constructed, that a translation of it was played in London, some years since, with prodigious success, without Halévy's, or any other music.

Gaetano Donizetti, born at Bergamo in 1798, only four years after Rossini, was rather the consequence, or reflex, than the rival of that gifted master. He has exhibited taste, facility, intelligence, and orchestral skill. Of his numerous dramatic productions, by far the greater number will, it is certain, never again see the light. On the other hand, his "L'Elisir d'Amore," "Lucrezia Borgia," and "Lucia di Lammermoor," are, after thirty years, still in the repertory of every existing lyric theatre. Donizetti however has been heard, like most contemporary dramatic composers of whatever nation, to the best advantage on the French stage. His grand opera "La Favorite," and his "opéra comique" "La Fille du Régiment," would of themselves have established a high reputation for him in both departments of the lyric drama.

If unequal in vigour or versatility to either of his fore-named compatriots, the Sicilian, Vincenzo Bellini, born 1802, rivals even the first in the sweetness and spontaneity of his melody, and surpasses both in refinement. In fecundity he was assuredly their inferior; but, on the other hand, of the very small number of his productions, two at least have outlived the great lyric artists for whom they were written, and to whom they were long said to be chiefly indebted for their success. Pasta, Grisi, Rubini, Tamburini, and Lablache, have all passed from the scene; but "La Sonnambula," and "Norma," keep their hold on public favour. Even the weaker "Puritani," when interpreted by competent artists, is still able to give pleasure. Bellini died in 1835, in his thirty-fourth year, regretted as much for the sweetness of his disposition and manners, as for the refined simplicity of his musical genius.

The successful example of Reinhard Keyser as a composer of German operas, in the beginning of the last century, did not, as I have already said, find many imitators among his countrymen. Graun and Hasse wrote and sang in scarcely any but Italian operas. Winter's name is never mentioned but in connexion with his "Ratto di Proserpina." Gluck's celebrity is exclusively due to his connexion with the French stage. Mozart indeed, the versatile Mozart, recommenced, though he did not carry on, the work which had been in abeyance since the death of Keyser, and in "Die Enthfürung aus dem Serail," and "Die Zauberflöte," proved that it might be made attractive still. But the majority of his librettos were Italian, set for and first interpreted by, Italian singers. Beethoven, in a single essay, gave proof of the versatility of his gigantic powers, but not with such success as to encourage him in making another. Spohr and Hummel added little to their great reputations by their connexion with the operatic stage, though the operas of the former master contain some of the most beautiful and popular of his vocal productions. Not till the present century had nearly completed its first quarter, did a German composer find for a musical drama, German in its subject, diction and musical treatment, success instantaneous, unequivocal and universal. In the year 1822 Carl Maria von Weber, born in 1786, produced at Berlin his opera "Der Freischütz." But this success, as it had been its composer's first, so it proved to be his last. The *magna*, or *major*, *pars* of every lyric drama, a libretto at once interesting in its subject and effectively planned, never again fell to the share of this gifted genius, who combined, perhaps in more perfect proportions than any other whom the world has yet known, the musical and the dramatic faculty. "Der Freischütz" may be a somewhat incoherent drama, but its subject is in the highest degree stimulating, its personages are sharply contrasted, and it presents several situations of commanding interest. But of

"Euryanthe" the leading idea is unpleasing and the treatment clumsy. Why the librettist did not adhere more closely to the conduct of his obvious model "Cymbeline" is hard to understand. The English "Oberon" is elegantly written and, like "Der Freischütz," presents some striking situations, which Weber has not failed to turn to account. But the subject wants human interest; and the work, despite its wealth of musical idea, set off by orchestration as varied, tender or gorgeous as the hues of an Eastern sunset, cannot be said to have attained more than a "succès d'estime."

Whether from the irregularity of his early training, or that his musical genius was of that kind which requires the stimulus of external circumstances, Weber was less successful in the symphonic than in the operatic style. His best instrumental pieces—his Concert-Stücke for example—are not so much concertos, sonatas, rondos or the like, as operas, or operatic scenes, without words. He has, however, raised to the dignity of a great work of art, a class of musical productions which, under inferior hands, had deserved no better name than that of *pot-pourri*. The overture to "Der Freischütz" is largely, and that of "Oberon" all but entirely, made up of passages from the operas which follow them; so welded together however, that in the result we have two of the most consequent and coherent compositions in existence. The career of this great genius was prematurely brought to an end in 1826. He died, in London, at the early age of thirty-nine.

The French musical drama owes its origin to Italian genius, its consolidation to German. Lully, as we have seen, a native of Florence, was not only its founder, but, even after a career of average duration, its ruler and its type. His immediate successor was Rameau, now chiefly remembered as a theorist, whose first attempt at opera was made in 1732, when he had attained the ripe age of forty-nine. His subsequent career, in spite of an inauspicious as well as a late commencement, was both prosperous and long. He lived till 1764, eighty-one years.

The music of Rameau, not less dramatic than that of Lully, more masculine in its design, and more interesting in its details, succeeded, with much difficulty, first in pleasing and subsequently in improving the French taste in music; which indeed was, not many years after, to be operated upon by a much stronger hand, that of Christopher Gluck. The success of this composer in Paris was in some degree prepared by some performances of Italian operas given there by Italians in 1752. In the course of these the dramatic music of Leo, Pergolesi, and other masters of the Neapolitan school was heard for the first time in the French capital. Though these performances met with little apparent success, for the sojourn in Paris of "les Italiens" was very short, the large melody and pure harmony to which they had been introduced by them was not without its effect both on French musicians and the French public. The development of the so-called "opéra comique," a class of production in which the musicians of France have for nearly a century past worked with unequalled success, is attributed by all the historians of the French stage to the impetus given by these performances.

The repertory of the "opéra comique" is the result of the felicitous co-operation, altogether exceptional out of France, of dramatists and musicians of equal skill in their several departments. Their combined products have also resulted in the formation of a class of performer altogether unique. The Italian singer does not speak; his utterance is essentially musical. The German actor in rare instances only has shown himself able to sing. The singer who can speak and the actor who can sing is to be found only, as one of a class, on the French stage. From the year 1747, in which "Les Italiens" visited Paris, an unbroken line of native composers presents itself who, always interpreted by native performers, have made the French "opéra comique" independent of, though it has not rejected, all extraneous aid. Mondonville, J. J. Rousseau, P. M. Berton, Philidor, Monsigny, Grétry, Dalayrac, Gaveaux, Leseuer, Méhul, R. Kreutzer, H. M. Berton, Catel, Isouard, Boieldieu, Auber, Herold, A. Adam, the majority of whom have written operas which still keep the stage, are with one exception, Grétry (a Belgian), Frenchmen by birth, education and life.

But in the higher walks of the musical drama France has not been so independent. From the middle of the last century to our own time, French Grand Opera has often been the work of foreigners.

In the year 1774 the "Iphigénie" of Christopher Gluck, a German composer of Italian operas now utterly forgotten, and who had then attained his sixty-fourth year, was produced in Paris at the Grand Opera, or "Académie Royale de Musique," with extraordinary success. This opera was rapidly followed by others from the same hand, all characterized by excellence in one respect of the same kind—a direct application of musical form and colour to dramatic expression, heretofore unknown to the French or any other theatre. The arrival shortly after of Nicolo Piccinni, an Italian composer of deservedly great reputation (then in his forty-sixth year), brought about what has been subsequently known as "the war of the Gluckists and Piccinnists;" a war in which much ink, but happily no blood, was freely shed. In this war, the musical science and taste of the combatants in which were in inverse ratio to their literary skill, the victory fell to Gluck; and fell to him at least as much through his skill in diplomacy as in music. This however I cannot now follow up. Of the two composers the Italian was, I think, the greater scholar, the German the greater genius. Both however exercised a prodigious influence on French musical taste, and made possible subsequently the production of that magnificent series of operas which France owes to the later Italians, Cherubini, Spontini, Rossini and Donizetti;

to the German, Meyerbeer; and to her own children, the accomplished Halévy and the gifted Auber.

Of some of these I have already spoken. To one more I must, before we part, call your special attention; a musician, the number and excellence of whose works entitle him to a very high place among the masters of his art, and from whose instructions, indirectly if not directly, all contemporary artists have in some degree profited; the last great master of the once great school of Italy, Maria Luigi Carlo Zenobi Salvador Cherubini.

The life of this musician was prolonged beyond even musical average, to eighty-two years. He was born at Florence in the year 1760, and died, at Paris, in 1842. His musical education was begun, and very well begun, by his father, and completed by the celebrated Sarti (1730–1802), under whose care he was placed at the age of eighteen, and whose pupil he remained during four years. His first opera, "Quinto Fabio," was produced at Milan in 1780, and followed in rapid succession by others, the majority of which obtained great success. In 1785-6 he visited London, where he wrote and produced two operas at the theatre in the Haymarket. Shortly after this he made his first visit to Paris, where he was received with great favour by the Court, and whither, after another trip to Italy, he returned in 1788. From this time France became his adopted country, and Paris his home. For more than fifty subsequent years, by his compositions, his theoretical works, and his personal influence and instruction, Cherubini was the musical autocrat of France, almost of Europe; his autocracy surviving changes of dynasty of another kind, numerous without precedent in political history.

An autobiographical and chronological catalogue of the works of Cherubini was published in Paris in 1845. It is assuredly the most singular production of its kind in existence. As a mere record of the labours of an individual it is sufficiently remarkable; though instances of longevity and fecundity are numerous enough among musicians. It extends over sixty-six years; for Cherubini was a composer at thirteen, and did not cease to write till he was seventy-nine. It contains the titles of twenty-eight operas, eighteen grand masses, several oratorios, and an enormous number of minor works of every kind. But the catalogue is not so remarkable musically as politically. It presents a sort of abstract of the history of France during the most eventful period in history. Cherubini took up his residence in Paris in 1788, one year before the meeting of the States-General at Versailles.

In 1790 he began an opera, "Marguerite d'Anjou," for the theatre at the Tuileries. This he never finished. One of the most remarkable facts connected with the history of the French Revolution is that, during its most tremendous excesses, the public theatres, sixty-three in number, were never closed, and never empty, for a single night. Cherubini continued, therefore, the practice of his art as a dramatic composer without cessation. One of his best works, "Lodoiska," was produced in 1791; and in the same year he made his first essay as a political composer, by the contribution of three choruses to a piece called "La Mort de Mirabeau." During the years 1792 and 1793 he resided out of Paris, but contributed music to the majority of the national fêtes. In the catalogue appear the following titles of compositions of this time:—"Hymne du Panthéon," "Hymne à la Fraternité," "Chant pour le Dix Août," "Hymne et Marche Funèbre pour la Mort du Général Hoche," "Ode sur la Dix-huit Fructidor," "Le Salpêtre Républicain," "Hymne pour la Fête de la Reconnaissance."

Cherubini's music was never relished by Napoleon, one of whose peculiarities was a nervous horror of loud or even animated music. His favourite composer was Paisiello, whose sweet but feeble strains presented perhaps the greatest contrast to anything in his own nature and pursuits that the world could furnish. The name of the First Consul does not appear in the Catalogue of Cherubini's works; but an "Ode pour le Mariage de *l'Empereur*" just indicates the moment when the sun was in its zenith. A few pages more bring us to 1814. Certain "morceaux militaires, composés pour l'Usage de la Musique du Régiment Prussien commandé par le Colonel Witzleben," mark the occupation of Paris by the Allies; and a cantata composed for a fête, "donnée par MM. les Officiers Supérieurs de la Garnison de Paris à la Garde Nationale et à MM. les Gardes-du-corps de sa Majesté, le 20 Juillet;" followed by another, "exécutée devant sa Majesté pendant la Fête donnée par la Ville de Paris, le 29 Août," tell their own story. The Hundred Days could hardly, with decency, call Cherubini's talents into requisition. But in August, 1815, royalty is again welcomed in certain "Couplets;" and a "Messe Solennelle" is begun in January, 1816, "pour la Chapelle du Roi." In the same year the marriage of "Monseigneur le Duc de Berri" is marked by a cantata; and from this time the frequent appearance of the words "Service de la Chapelle" records the continuance of political tranquillity or torpor. The last of these entries is of a motet for Quinquagesima Sunday, 1829. The revolution of 1830 left him his most important post, that of Director of the Conservatoire; and shortly before his death he was named "Commandeur de la Légion d'Honneur," by Louis Philippe. But he does not appear to have composed for the new dynasty, which, though itself not very long-lived, survived *him*.

I have now, so far as time has permitted, completed my outlines of the musical history of the past; it only remains for me to say a few words about the music *of the future*. I am not going to indulge myself, at the expense of your time and patience, in prophecy, nor even in speculation. But many of you will know that, in the classic land of modern music, Germany, a school of poets and prophets has sprung up which has undertaken to tell us what the music of the future is to be. Not only so. This school is so impatient for the realization of its own prognostications, that it has actually brought a good deal of this music into the world, as it might seem, considerably before its time. Some of it too is already, and a good deal of it seems likely soon to be, forgotten. So that it would seem to combine the somewhat impossible conditions of being past and present, as well as future. Leaving its progenitors, however, to reconcile this confusion of tenses, I will endeavour to explain their theory, so far as I understand it.

To say the truth, there is not much in this at which anybody will be likely seriously to take exception. It amounts to this; that the world has not yet seen a work of art to the production of which the poet, the painter, the musician, and the stage-manager have contributed with equal energy and success; that such a work is possible; and that, being achieved, it would at once restore poetry to its ancient influence on the feelings and the actions of mankind, turn painting to a thoroughly practical account, and transform music, from the mere amusement of an idle hour, into a vehicle for communicating the noblest impulses and exciting to the noblest deeds. The chief preacher of this philosophy, Herr Richard Wagner, repudiates, or till lately repudiated, for himself and his disciples, the term "music of the future," as a misrepresentation both of his words and his views; which latter are more properly and fully rendered, he says, by the more comprehensive term "work of art of the future."

Now, had the theory of a "work of art of the future" been put before the world as a simple proposition, it would have been received with a good deal of respectful consideration; especially from those who knew little of the history of music, and the limits or conditions of the musical art. The proposition is by no means a new one, and the *idea* of which it is the expression is as old as the drama, of whatever species, of modern times. It is the idea which governed the "mysteries" of the Middle Ages; it is the idea which haunted the Florentine Academy in their search after the musical declamation of the ancients; it is the idea which tormented the composers of the Third Period, one and all; and *the* idea, the *one* idea, of Gluck. It is impossible to deny that it is a good idea. But there is a condition connected with it, sometimes avowed, sometimes held in reserve, against which the instincts of humanity have so far rebelled; that its realization would involve the calling into existence of a new kind of music, and the interruption of that process of gradual development to which the musical art has submitted for the past five hundred and fifty years, certainly with results not unsatisfactory to mankind.

This it might have been difficult to prove, had the musicians "of the future" abstained from carrying their theories into practice, and presenting abstract ideas in the concrete form of musical composition. I have never had an opportunity of witnessing the performance of one of Herr Wagner's operas. I made a great effort, a few weeks since,* to be present when one of them, "Tannhauser," was produced in Paris, with all the care, and cost, and forethought which so eminently distinguish productions of this kind in the Académie Impériale. It was withdrawn after a third performance, for which I did not arrive in time. But I have the same acquaintance with this work that every musician has with nineteen-twentieths of the music with which he is acquainted; that which is derived from study and perusal. I find in the pieces of which "Tannhauser" is composed, an entire absence of musical construction and coherence; little melody, and that of a most unoriginal and *mesquin* kind; and harmony chiefly remarkable for its restless, purposeless, and seemingly helpless modulation. Lully, the founder of French opera, was complained of, even in the height of his popularity, for the extent to which he carried recitative

* In 1862.

and "aria parlante;" forms, in good hands, capable of agreeable effect in themselves, and allowing opportunity to the ear to repose from the fatigue engendered by too long continued, or too strongly accentuated, rhythm. Wagner *out-Lullies* Lully, and allows the persons of his drama "of the future" to discourse about the past, at a length and in a language which show a wonderful want of understanding of the patience of any but a Wagnerian auditory. Were these things found in an ordinary opera, one would simply dismiss it as a very indifferent and a very tiresome opera. But they are matters of faith and of principle with the new school. Dulness, ugliness and want of form are justified by all sorts of analogies which, true or false, are no consolation to those who suffer under them. Nature, we are told, is not always interesting, lovely or symmetrical; she is very often dull; *ergo*, art should not be always lively. The answer to all this is almost too obvious to be given. We endure dulness as best we can, when there is no escape from it; but no one seeks it or tolerates it, that can choose his occupation or his company.

Music—I mean the music of the present—as compared with every other fine art, is yet young: it is possible and probable that she has powers yet undeveloped, yet even untried. The type of what we now understand by, and expect to find in, Opera is hardly a century old; and perhaps no example of that "work of art" is yet before the world which, in some respect, is not open to exception. It would be impertinent and unsafe to dogmatize about any "work of art" which shall be accepted as perfect by a more critical generation than our own; but I will venture to say that it will present no such evidences of contempt for the Music of the Past as are presented in that of the Future of which we have been favoured with specimens, at the present time. The connexion between one age and another is no more to be suddenly broken off with impunity in art than in anything else. Change, whether by aggregation, rejection or growth, is no doubt a condition of life; but it is itself subject to another condition, that it be gradual, gentle, and unostentatious.

The music of the future may be safely left to grow out of the music of the present, as the music of the present has grown out of the music of the past. An altogether new kind of music may not be an impossibility; it will be long ere it need become a necessity. I most firmly believe that the resources of the art, as we understand it, are not only unexhausted but inexhaustible.

POSTSCRIPT.

LONDON, *June*, 1875.

WAGNER'S opera, "Lohengrin," long promised and long waited for, has, years after this course of lectures was brought to an end, been performed in London at both our great lyric theatres. I subjoin a paper which embodies my impression of the result of these performances, from which I omit only a few passages of altogether temporary interest.

Such frequent and pressing calls have been made of late on the attention of musical amateurs by the disciples of Wagner, his intentions have been so thoroughly expounded, and his performances so widely advertised, that there can now be no necessity for even the briefest exposition of a theory which some hold to be new and not true, others true and not new, and others neither new nor true. That any kind of art characterised neither by freshness nor beauty should, as the art of Wagner has assuredly for some time past done, engage the attention and largely win the admiration of musical Europe would be incredible, did we not know to what extent, and with what unerring certainty, success may be won for any cause or for anything, the advocacy of which is sufficiently loud and long continued. Such advocacy too, it is fair to say, as the Wagnerian theory has found, not merely in its birthplace but among ourselves, and even in the south of Europe, has been both honest and intelligent; nor is it possible to deny that the Wagnerian sect—for such it may now be fairly called—has drawn within its pale many who, both by their musical science and their general intelligence, have a right to hold an opinion on a musical question and to express it. But advocacy, like opposition, is, after all, limited in its action on great artists or great art. Either may incline opinion, especially in the direction it would have taken for itself. But it can only do even this for a season. Sooner or later—too often later than can be pleasant or profitable to the artist—the ultimate court of appeal, the great public, takes the pending cause out of the hands of pleaders on both sides, and settles it for ever. How it will settle the "cause Wagnerienne" in its entirety remains to be seen. This much is certain that, with whatever amount of intemperance the Wagnerian idea may have been advocated, the germ of truth which it contains will

"Live and act and serve the future hour."

The art against which its advocates wage war may not deserve all the hard usage it has met with at their hands; but it is not impeccable; and its practitioners are more likely to ascertain in what its peccability consists from its enemies than from its friends. The opera of Wagner may not take the place of the opera of Mozart, of Rossini, of Meyerbeer, or of Verdi, but the opera of the next musician of genius will be very different from what it would have been had Wagner never lived.

"Lohengrin" may be said to belong to its composer's second period; and its products, like those of another very different composer's second period, have so far proved the most acceptable to the world. "Rienzi" and even "Der Fliegende Holländer," are avowedly the work of a "'prentice hand;" and his more recent productions, whatever their inherent merit or attractiveness, are on too great a scale to be practicable, save in a few places, and even in these on rare occasions. But in "Lohengrin" the Wagnerian type is sufficiently developed to admit of fair investigation; and in assisting at its performance we are in a condition to judge how far in opera what has hitherto been regarded as Music can to a large extent be dispensed with, and action carried on by means of one only, and that the least delightful kind of music—"aria parlante." Aria parlante, it should be observed, attained to an approximately perfect form long before every other kind of music. Specimens of it, which for just expression and even musical beauty it would be hard even now to equal, abound in the writings of many musicians of the seventeenth century whose views of melody, harmony, and form were limited and uncertain. And this from the simple cause that its production demands rather susceptibility to poetical impressions than musical science or even musical feeling. Large use of "aria parlante" in an opera, therefore, is not now-a-days progress, but regress; and the composer who uses it to the exclusion of other kinds of music lays himself open to the charge of want of ability to turn *them* to account. Whether this charge can fairly be laid to Wagner is not, however, the question before us. This is rather, whether in "Lohengrin" he has produced a work which, when the passions which have been raised about it and its author have subsided, will continue to give such pleasure as it seems to give at the present moment.

* * * * * * *

The "poem" Lohengrin is the work of the composer, whose powers as a master of language are at least as highly esteemed by many of his countrymen as his music. Every opera loses, and a Wagnerian opera more than any other, by translation; and the "poet" of that before us must not be judged by the Italian words which are made the interpreters of his thoughts, and the "vehicle" of his music. But the subject and plan of "Lohengrin" are revealed to us in the performances at Drury Lane intact; and to both of these we have to make serious objection. Whether "the old Teutonic myths," about which we have heard so much lately, and to which Wagner seems now to be exclusively devoted, can ever excite more than a national interest is a question. Whether any myth can may be doubted. A great poet, also an admirable critic—Lord Byron—has laid down a law that the basis of drama must be history. "There should always be," says he, "some foundation for the most airy fabric; pure invention is but the talent of a liar." Then the plan or construction of "Lohengrin" violates the first law of dramatic construction. Things are *told* which ought to be *done;* and things are *done* which ought to be *told*. The long explanation, in the last scene, of Lohengrin's antecedents might have been made unnecessary by a prelude, in which the audience, though not the *dramatis personæ,* would have made acquaintance with Parcival and his peers, Monsalvato and the Sangraal—personages, a place, and a thing of which they know nothing, and in which they cannot possibly have any interest. On the other hand, the arrival of the hero, *viâ* the Scheldt —usually much encumbered with craft—in a boat just large enough to contain him, and drawn by a swan, is an incident which skilful treatment might make interesting in narrative, but which no treatment could have made otherwise than ridiculous in dramatic action. With the music of "Lohengrin" we did not of course make first acquaintance on Saturday night; but we have always hesitated even to form, still more to express, an opinion of its merits, apart from the drama to which it belongs, and of which avowedly it is but one element. Of this drama, "Lohengrin," presented in music, we are constrained to say that, in spite of a power of realizing to himself dramatic situation, in which perhaps Wagner is unprecedented; in spite of individual passages, here of energy, there of sweetness; in spite of orchestral effects as astonishing for their beauty as for their freshness and variety, we find "Lohengrin"—dull. It will attract for a time. The curiosity raised in respect to it makes it natural and to be desired that it should do so. But that works after the manner of "Lohengrin," which—accepting the word "music" in the sense for some centuries past given to it—may be described as *operas without music*, should take any permanent hold on the human soul, is to us simply inconceivable.